A·N·G·E·L·S  I·N
O·U·R  M·I·D·S·T

Other Books by Mary Fisher:

*Sleep With the Angels*
*I'll Not Go Quietly*
*My Name Is Mary*

# A·N·G·E·L·S IN
# O·U·R M·I·D·S·T

Photographs and Text by

*Mary Fisher*

*Chuck,*
*With love,*
*Mary F 98*

Moyer Bell
Wakefield, Rhode Island & London

Published by Moyer Bell

Copyright © 1997 by Family AIDS Network, Inc. [501(c)(3)]

Photographs Copyright © 1997 by Mary Fisher

First Edition

LIBRARY OF CONGRESS
CATALOGING IN PUBLICATION DATA

Fisher, Mary, 1948-
    Angels in our midst / by Mary Fisher. —1st ed.

    p.                      cm.
    1. AIDS (Disease). 2. AIDS (Disease)—Social
    aspects. 3. AIDS (Disease)—United States.
    I. Title.
    RC607.A26F549                       1997
    362.1'969792—dc21                   97-33427
    isbn: 1-55921-218-7 (cloth)         CIP

Printed in Mexico
Distributed in North America by Publishers Group West,
P.O. Box 8843, Emeryville CA 94662 800-788-3123 (in
California 510-658-3453) and in Europe by Gazelle Book
Services Ltd., Falcon House, Queen Square, Lancaster LA1
1RN England 524-68765.

Jacket photograph (front) of Colleen Haley at Connor's Nursery, West Palm Beach, Florida
Jacket photograph (back) by Dirck Halstead of Mary Mider and Mary Fisher in Washington, D.C.
Half title: (l to r) Connor's Nursery, Project Open Hand, Tuesday's Child, Common Ground
Title page: Jacqueline and Stephen Sullivan, Haven House, Atlanta

To Michael Saag
Physician, Researcher, Cousin, and Caregiver.
Who taught me that science without love is lifeless, and
that great healers never deny the grief—they are merely
undefeated by it.

# CONTENTS

*Foreword*                9

*Acknowledgments*         13

Grand Rapids             16

Boston                   26

Atlanta                  40

Rikers Island            50

West Palm Beach          58

New York City            64

Gallery of Caregivers    77

Kansas City              86

San Francisco            94

Los Angeles              104

Washington, D.C.         114

Birmingham               130

*Program Profiles*        144

# FOREWORD

I'm not sure what I had in mind when I decided to start taking photographs of caregivers, but it wasn't a book. It might have been a wall full of photographs, like the famous AIDS Quilt, that would tell a story in each image. I wasn't certain. But I knew I wanted to focus on caregivers, those people who bring us extraordinary compassion during our life's most vulnerable times. The only thing not clear was how to capture and tell their stories.

Working in the White House and, before that, in television studios, I'd met famous people ranging from Soupy Sales, a favored guest on a show I had produced in Detroit, to Henry Kissinger, who may be as different from Soupy Sales as one male can be from another. I'd been raised in a home where powerbrokers were father's friends, where my mother charmed movie stars and dignitaries. I'd traveled with a president as he wrestled with global issues. I'd seen egos of spectacular dimensions and even met a few saints.

But for pure human power, no set of people are as extraordinary as the caregivers who come, most of them unpaid, to help us manage our lives when life itself grows fragile and fearful. They are, collectively, an almost entirely invisible army of compassion. Individually, they are heroes of unrivaled proportion who—in city after city, time after time—told me, "I'm not doing anything special." They are so perfectly unselfconscious that they do not know their own staggering goodness.

Entering the room of someone wrestling with death is an act of invasion. These are intimate places shrouded with vulnerability and mystery. To come in carrying a camera seems sacrilegious. My sensitivity may have been heightened by my own diagnosis with a disease regarded as terminal, so that when I meet someone needing care I am looking into a mirror of my own future. But the overwhelming sense of these places is less of illness than of heroism displayed by those who've come not as chroniclers but as comforters: the father who held his stranger-son's hand as it grew cool. . .the grandmother who whispered away the fears of the grandson she adored. . .the doctor who loved, and did not leave, those he could not heal. Compassionate caregiving is almost beyond imagination, even after you've encountered it first-hand.

This happens to be a collection featuring caregivers of persons with AIDS, the disease that already has ended hundreds of thousands of American lives and is destroying millions more. But those pictured here would care for others no matter what disease they suffered, especially the disease of moral judgmentalism that still attaches itself like a festering sore to the American AIDS epidemic and which stands in sharp contrast to the dignified compassion and amazing grace poured out by every caregiver I've met. Many are contributing to programs that I have high-lighted in the last chapter called "Program Profiles." These programs are a few of thousands like them around the country and the world. And I'm grateful to have spent time with each of them.

Much has changed in the American AIDS epidemic since it first broke through two decades ago, and since my own HIV-positive diagnosis in 1991. Americans have grown weary of the epidemic. The media don't cover it as much or in the same way as they once did. How can a story that has remained fundamentally unchanged for two decades still be news? For a while, new drug therapies generated scores of headlines and fueled the misperception that a cure had been found. It hadn't. And while the headlines crowed about hope, the real story remained the same. It is still about dying.

Into this story come the heroes of this book—and my heroes, too—caregivers. When I ask if I may take their pictures, they wonder why. When I say they are the angels in our midst, they shake their heads in disbelief. They would be the last, the very last, to think of themselves as heroic.

But if you've measured your own mortality, you've encountered some hard and doubting questions: Who will be there at the end, especially if it comes slowly? Who will demand that our pain be lessened, or soothe our lips with ice? Who will shepherd us through our terrors? Who will be patient with us, and treat us to the dignity we have lost? Sooner or later, a caregiver will be needed by each of us either to answer our hardest questions or to tell us the answers don't really matter.

Caregivers may appear when least we expect them. I was working through this book and through despondency at the same time. In public I said my depression was a side effect of prescriptions. Privately, I knew better. Being sick hadn't helped, but neither had it started my depression. Long before I changed drug regimens I'd been sinking toward the belief that life didn't matter any more. I felt useless, and tired, and especially lonesome. Around my children, I tried to put on a happy face. When they were gone, so was that face.

And then came Suzie Schomaker, a friend. She pulled out her guitar and taught me new songs. She reminded me that intimacy requires trust, not hiding; that laughter really is the best medicine; and that accepting love may be harder for some of us than giving it. She talked and listened and hugged her way around the walls I'd built up. And, in the process, she joined the ranks of caregivers cited here.

Pure caregiving requires us to give up the silly notion that we are independent or self-sufficient. Of course, we are not. None of us. Ever. We are irrevocably dependent on others. We embrace each other in care because we know that, alone, we cannot survive. The essence of caregiving is love.

My son Zachary turned eight as this book went to press, a week after his brother Max turned ten. In loving me, they care for me, which is how I also care for them.

And with this book I can hand them evidence that we are not alone. In the photos and text spread across these pages, I can prove to them that—even if I should one day be gone—there are heroes who will step forward. Always. Everywhere.

Mary Fisher
*Yom Kippur, 1997*

# ACKNOWLEDGMENTS

Jennifer Moyer and Britt Bell, who worked with me on my first book, *Sleep With the Angels*, won not only my respect but also my affection. During our first discussion of this book, they promised to donate all profits to the Family AIDS Network. Like members of my family—especially my parents, Max and Marjorie Fisher—they've constantly looked beyond the hard and painful issues to find good people and good lessons.

Carvin Winans is a member of the world-famous and five-time Grammy-winning gospel singing group, The Winans. Since we met a year ago, he and his family (especially his wife, Debbie) have become great friends and important colleagues in the fight against AIDS.

Some years ago David Hume Kennerly urged me to take my camera more seriously. Dirck Halstead accompanied me while I photographed caregivers. I could not have had better mentors.

While I was busy with this book, Sheila McGovern and Dillon Whitlock managed details of daily living at home. I sorted negatives and prints while the world's best sister-in-law, Tina Campbell, pointed out that "this place goes nuts when you do a book" and did what she could to maintain normalcy. Staff at Mary Fisher Productions in Nyack, New York, carried on in my absence. Pat Jones taught me to play the guitar, despite lessons I canceled and rescheduled. Ann Cullen patiently fielded calls I couldn't answer. And Steve Gunderson and his colleagues at The Greystone Companies carried the weight of the Family AIDS Network. I'm grateful to them all.

Every caregiver in my life is extraordinary. A few of them must be named: Rosie O'Donnell, because friendship is more important to her than fame; members of The All Girls Band, because they've reminded me how much fun it is to play; the San Francisco Giants, because they joined the fight against AIDS and did not leave when it was no longer a fad; A. James Heynen and Lizbeth Leeson, because they love me; Suzie Schomaker, because she lifted my soul with her songs; and, always and above all others, my sons, Max and Zachary—because they give me a reason not only to live, but to live with integrity.

Carlo Pinna with
Zack and Max Fisher

A·N·G·E·L·S  I·N
O·U·R  M·I·D·S·T

# GRAND RAPIDS
## November 1993

Jan Koopman convinced people to trust me. To do it, she drew on the local respect she had earned by transforming the Grand Rapids (Michigan) AIDS Resource Center into a place of compassionate service.

Five months earlier I had lain with Brian as he died in his bedroom in Massachusetts. I'd flown from Boston to Detroit to tell our sons, Max and Zack, that "Daddy died this morning," Father's Day, 1993.

Now it was nearing Thanksgiving, the first of the winter holidays, the first holiday in which the boys would have no father. Between June and November I'd decided to take photographs of caregivers, to show the outside world the faces of the heroes who live among us.

Jan was driving and talking about the food bank, our first stop. She was rehearsing our itinerary for two days of visits, explaining who would be where, warning me about this staff person or that family member who hadn't wanted anyone taking pictures, worrying that Kevin or Andy might die before we could get to them.

When she admitted fearing that death would arrive before we did,

I made a mental journey back to Brian's apartment, to his sister-care-giver, Tina, to the priest who came to anoint him that last Saturday, to the all-night vigils during which I lay next to him, listening to him breathe, wanting him to find comfort without dying.

I wouldn't have wanted anyone taking pictures.

My splendid idea, to let the world see caregivers at work, suddenly seemed crude. How could I capture the terrible intimacy of these moments without violating it? How could I get an image of the relationship between the caregivers and the people for whom they care? It was too late, now, not to take photographs. But what had been such a good idea earlier, when I was planning the trip and loading the film, was obviously a mistake.

**Food Bank**. We stopped at a food bank where people were preparing meals to take to persons with AIDS. I wanted to take pictures; people wanted to talk to me. I was juggling cameras and handshakes. The lens fogged up when we came in from the cold. Lighting was awful and I didn't know what kind of film might work. There was no time to set up, no time to sort of hide in the corner and get an idea of what to shoot. They were waiting for me when I got there. They wanted to pose. I wanted to be invisible and gifted. I was neither.

**Rock's House**. As if Rock's body had not suffered enough with AIDS, he'd also endured another round of chemotherapy. He was sick

*May 10, 1996*
*Dear Mary,*

*I know now that the greatest honor we can receive is to be told that someone trusts us enough to ask that we assist them in dying. I see it as a spiritual time, to be able to send someone off to their next life in comfort and love. I've received the gift twice. I feel selfish.*
*F. V.*
*Rhode Island*

when we arrived. The room was dark. He told me how grateful he was for the support of his friend, Steve. They sat on the couch together and talked. But his eyes told me that his greatest caregiver—the one he trusts most, the one he fears someone will take from him before he dies—is Abby. "She's still a puppy," he said. Rock and Steve wanted a picture of me with Abby. I think I was crying.

**<u>Home of Hope Hospice</u>**. Andy Dilay's caregiver, his sister Jackie, spoke to me by speaking to Andy: "Andy, remember when you were in a coma and I asked if you wanted to meet Mary Fisher?" I thought, at first, that she was humoring him, like a mother talking to a three-year-old. But then he nodded. "Remember how important it was to you?" He nodded, eyes closed. She took his hand, turned to me, and said, "I think that maybe when he and I talked about this, they said he was in a coma but I think he heard it, and I think he came out of his coma for this. Do you think so, Andy?"

She told me about his Russian teacher ("He comes to see you every week, doesn't he, Andy?"). She said Andy was fluent in Russian, and was still learning new words.

These people had lived vibrant, vigorous lives before they knew the meaning of a hospice. I wanted to learn everything about them so I could tell the world his story, and hers. What had he been like as a little boy? How had she grown so strong and loving? Whom had he trusted, and whom had she left to be with him?

Andy Dilay and
Jackie Donehoo

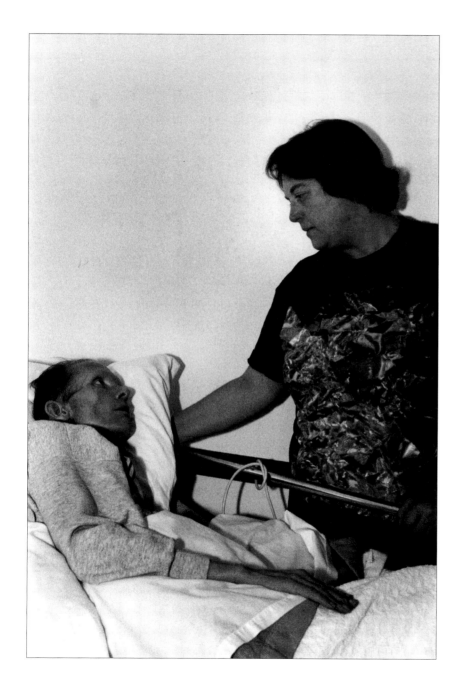

By the time I'd opened cases and adjusted a camera, found an angle and moved around the room once or twice, I had no time to ask questions. But it wasn't just time that I lacked. I couldn't get comfortable with asking for more. My cameras made me feel as if I were already an intruder. And if I asked a question of Jackie so she'd turn to answer, she would be staring into a camera's lens. It felt awkward.

Everything here was intimate: the gentle touches, Jackie's voice, the dying, and the caring for someone dying. The clicking of the camera was too loud. When the film rolled, the whirring seemed never to end. I was grateful when Jackie spoke, when she demanded that Andy be involved with us by including him in every sentence. He was not to be left out, not to be discussed as if he were absent or incompetent. By speaking only in questions and letting him nod, she not only affirmed his reality in her life and mine, she gave him a voice. Her voice.

I never learned why he spoke Russian.

**Sherri**. She had lost her brother to AIDS "a few months ago, this summer. It was hot." Now she had adopted two others to care for, Jessie and Doug, both fighting the virus that had felled her brother.

"It's hard to stop once you get started," she explained when I asked why she did this. "I don't know. It's just something I need to do."

## Hospice of Greater Grand Rapids at Kent Community Hospital. It smelled like a hospital. The elevator to the fifth floor made hospital noises.

Jan Koopman told me that Kevin Donnally had decided I should come and take pictures. From Jan's tone of voice, I wondered if his family had opposed it. She didn't say.

When I opened the door to Kevin's room, his mother stood up from the side of his bed and came to hug me. We talked for a moment, she introduced me to her husband, and then said, "the rest of the family's down the hall." Kevin was coughing. She went back to hold him.

The Donnally family was from Detroit but "we came when Kevin got sick," said his mother. First it had been Kevin and his mother, then his father had joined them, and now the whole family was there, including Kevin's brothers and their wives.

Jesús Cruz and Sherri Homan

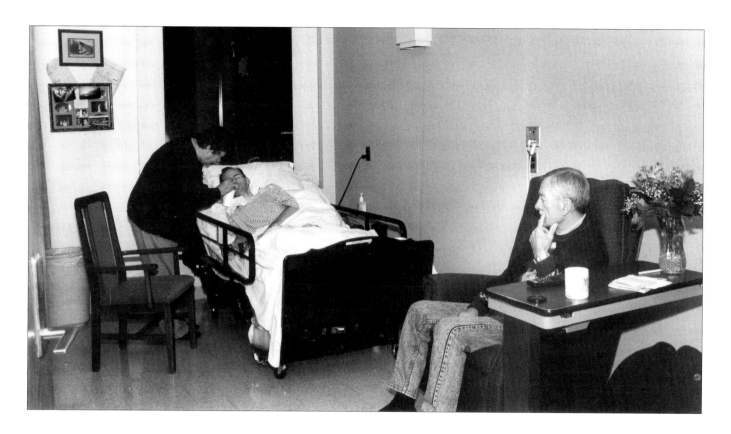

Rita and Jim Donnally
with son, Kevin

I moved around as quietly as I could, but the room was small. I was noisy. My cameras and I were foreigners here.

Kevin's mother talked as I shot film. She said that her husband was a retired Detroit police officer, and now her sons were on the force. I asked if they knew Joe Arita, a retired policeman who had been helpful to my family years ago when there had been some threats. They did. It created an immediate bond between us—strangers, in a room dominated by a deathbed, stumbling into the realization that we shared other parts of our lives before this night.

Kevin couldn't speak anymore, but he was responsive to his mother and, later, to me. I leaned toward him to put our faces close to each other. I told him I understood, and that he was loved very much, and that his life was so important. He knew.

For a sergeant, his rank at retirement, Kevin's father seemed fragile and gray. His sons down the hall looked more like police officers: huskier, intimidating. Their father sat in a chair, holding his chin with his left hand, his right hand dangling. He appeared deep in thought, sad, old.

When I was ready to go, Mrs. Donnally asked if I would step out with her for a moment. I expected her to ask that I not use some of the photographs. "How are you doing?" she asked, almost affectionately. I told her I was doing well.

Then she asked about my parents. "This is different than you think it will be," she said, "harder than you can imagine." And she asked again how my parents were

Chris Holland and Peggy Hudson

doing. I told her my parents weren't really talking about my diagnosis very much. She nodded. "Sure. . .sure. . . ." Her voice trailed off. "We were like that, too," she said, coming back to the present. "I remember."

"Tell your mother she can call me," she said. "I'll be there for her. I understand."

❧ EXCERPT ❧

*Let me tell you what I found this past Wednesday evening. I found a hospice here, in this city, full of joy and compassion, full of love. Most of the patients were old—until I came to those with AIDS. They were young.*

*And there I met Andy. Brilliant, brilliant Andy, fluent in English and in Russian, now unable to speak in any language at all. When I held his hand and looked down, I felt the waxy cold and saw the telltale blue beneath his fingernails. He was wasting away, but even starvation takes time.*

*"He's so young," said his sister, "and his heart is so strong. It won't let him die."*

*I wasn't prepared for this. I'd gone to the hospice as a photographer, to shoot pictures for an upcoming series on caregivers.*

*But when I took up Andy's hand, I could not put it down. When I saw the eyes of his sister, I could only weep.*

*I am grateful for the philanthropies that have supported this hospice. But what I thought when I lay sleepless Wednesday night was this: If professionalism in philanthropy enables us to support such work but keeps us from experiencing it, we who are most financially wealthy are at risk of being most spiritually impoverished.*

*Excerpt from*
*"A Tale of Two Families"*
*Address by Mary Fisher*
*Council of Michigan Foundations*
*Annual Conference*
*Grand Rapids, Michigan*
*Friday, November 5, 1993*

# BOSTON
November 1993

Dying is not pretty and rarely graceful. Only on Hollywood sets is it clean and odorless. If we die slowly enough to have others care for us near the end, it's a physical struggle that involves a mean betrayal by our own bodies. First we lose control, then we lose dignity, then we lose life, more or less in that order.

The extraordinary power of the caregivers I've met is in the ways they find to give back what our bodies take from us. They see to it, in amazingly detailed and tangible ways, that the person whose hours are numbered stays in charge of pain killers, of color schemes and music choices, of who comes and who's barred from coming. When the coughing spells lead to spurts of vomit, when bowels and bladders empty without warning, caregivers are neither surprised nor offended. I've heard them say, with quiet grace and good cheer, "I'm so glad you got that out; you'll feel better now." Love is not sanitized in this setting. It is gritty, unquestioned, and spectacular.

At the hour of passing, when the body has forfeited everything except the soul, caregivers keep alive the spark of life while waiting for

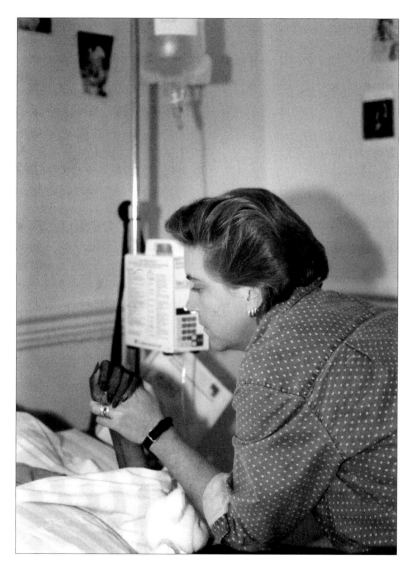

Kate Ryan

the quiet peace to come, and then they focus on the peace not as an ending (blessed as that might seem) but as a confirmation of life. I've heard their soothing words, watched them cradle a dying man. They enable us to treasure life on either side of death. I once put down my camera because it seemed indecent to photograph something so holy as an elderly woman, a caregiver of unrivaled affection, gently pushing back a shock of her grandson's thin hair.

I learned all this about caregivers in Boston in the year before I came back bearing a camera. Brian, the man with whom I'd shared marriage and children and AIDS, had moved home to the Boston area. It's where we had made peace with each other after years of seething distrust, where we worked in handmade paper and did art together, where we lay together as he died. It's where I marvelled as his sister Tina cared for him with both strength and patience. It's where I met Pat Gibbons and Manny Souza, who enabled me, for at least a little while, to join the ranks of caregivers.

**Rosie's Place**. I'd not been back to Boston since Brian's memorial service in late September. Pat Gibbons thought I should visit Rosie's Place, a community-based program for women who confront, among other brutal realities, AIDS.

Christyne Howard was one of those women. For years she'd known, and been known, on the streets of Boston. "Off-and-on sober and clean," one of the staff members said of Christyne. Since women needed to be drug-free to stay at Rosie's Place, Christyne had cleaned up her act for one final performance. And, in the process, she'd found a special place in the heart of Kate Ryan.

Kate is, by training and profession, a social worker; in fact, she's a caregiver. Her short, blonde hair and pretty features don't suggest a person familiar with death. But when she talks, you hear wisdom. I've never heard her use a long sentence. She measures life precisely, briefly. She takes charge in a few words spoken with quiet, unquestioned strength. It's gentle and caring, but intense, powerful.

*Kim had struggled all her life just to survive. Her experience of lack of care was typical for women with AIDS. But her story was more poignant because she had a child, a son, whom she loved desperately. She wanted to hold on to him, but knew he needed to plan for a future without her.*

*Mary Fisher called one day, said she was in town and wanted to drop by. It was Christmas time. She asked if there was anyone I wanted her to see or talk to. Kim.*

*I introduced them, Mary to Kim, thinking "here's where wealth and fame meet hard times and the street." In some ways, they couldn't have been more different. But I'll never forget watching Mary take Kim into her arms, hearing the soft, muffled sounds of two women sharing tears together as I closed the door.*

*I never knew what Kim and Mary talked about. After Mary left, a package came for Kim. It was a beautiful AIDS ribbon, like the one Mary sometimes wears. Kim wore the ribbon until she died. And then, on her instructions, she was buried with the pin and this note: "AIDS pin from my friend Mary."*

*Personal Correspondence from Pat Gibbons*
*June 26, 1997*

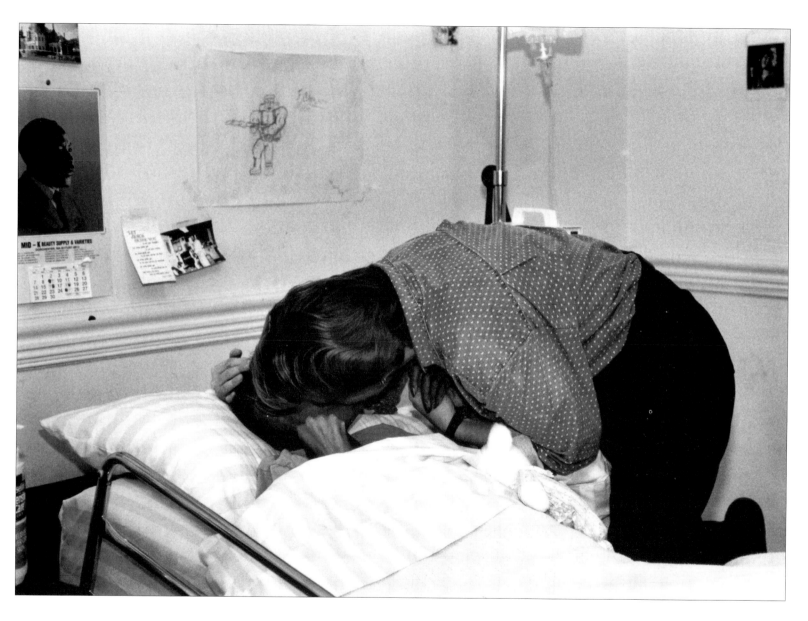

Christyne Howard and Kate Ryan

"Christyne's unforgettable," said Kate, already reconciling herself to Christyne's passing and the memories that would be left behind. She told me that she'd explained to Christyne the changes she needed to make if she wanted to stay at Rosie's Place. For all her emotional steel, Kate softened when describing Christyne's determined attempt to take charge of her own life and enrich the lives of her children. She remembered stories—some funny, most not. But she never spoke of Christyne in the language of social work; she never said "resident" or "client." It was always "Christyne," and the word carried a sense of elegance.

A year later I went back to give a luncheon speech for Rosie's Place. It was a fundraising event with a crowd full of celebrities, hosted by Lily Tomlin. I told them about Christyne and Kate.

**Children's AIDS Program.** When I arrived, they explained that they were not comfortable having me take photographs. I

*The first time I met Kate Ryan, she was leaning over Christyne's bed, talking softly. And when they let me into their conversation, I discovered they were talking about death.*

*Christyne had suffered the assaults of racism and sexism and, as the final insult, a virus that wanted to take away what dignity she had assembled. And the question she faced—not with dripping emotion but with great resolve—was: Where shall I die? She worried about who would be near to help and hold her children at that hour. And she worried about who would make the decisions when she was gone.*

*Rosie's Place is not a hospice. But Christyne thought that, if she could, she would prefer to die at Rosie's Place. And the deciding factor was unbelievably simple: This was the place where, after a too-short life of too-frequent abuse, she had tasted unbridled, unqualified love. In other places Christyne had learned not to tell people she was sick, because then they rejected her. But when she came home to Rosie's Place, they had embraced her with affection and steadied her children with courage. And, if she could, this was the place where she wanted to say "Good bye."*

*I took pictures while she talked. Then there was a moment of silence. And when I heard Kate say, "Yes, of course. Absolutely. I'd like that too. This would be a good place to die"—that's when I knew that Kate was no ordinary person, and this was no ordinary place, and that I had come home, too.*

*Excerpt from "Lunch with Lily and the Ladies"*
*Address by Mary Fisher*
*A Benefit for Rosie's Place*
*Boston, Massachusetts*
*Friday, October 28, 1994*

Margaret Jackson

was sorry, not so much for the photography as for the language they used. "These are just innocent victims," they said of the children here, all of them fighting AIDS. I bristled at the suggestion that the children were more deserving of love than Kevin or Andy or Christyne. I would have, I think, left angry. But I couldn't. Because I met Margaret Jackson, a teacher and a caregiver who was cuddling a child with the same passion that I'd cuddled Max and Zack. It wasn't pity that flowed through her strong arms or clear eyes. It was love—absolute, unflinching love.

She spoke softly, wanting not to rouse the child nearing sleep in her arms. "It doesn't discriminate, does it?" she said of AIDS. "We could learn something from that, couldn't we?"

**Mission Hill Hospice**. When I think hospice, I think Mission Hill. I visited first when the National Commission on AIDS was meeting in Boston and Mission Hill was a stop on our tour. I arrived late and Pat Gibbons, the remarkable woman who headed Mission Hill at the time, gave me a personal tour.

She explained hospice to me. "Let me show you this," she said as she swung open the door to an empty room. Next to a well-made bed, on a small nightstand, was a white bud vase in which a single, deep-pink rose, half-opened, was maintaining its vigil. "I wanted to show you this before you met others," said Pat, as she glided comfortably into the story of the woman who had died in the room the day before. "We don't just clean it out," she said.

Some months later, when I feared Brian was dying, I asked Pat to visit with us. We had tea together at a Boston hotel. I didn't know what to say to the children, or what to plan for myself, because Brian was bouncing between intensive care one week and rollerblading the next.

"What do you think?" I asked her the moment Brian excused himself for a break. It was the only time I've known Pat to appear uncertain. She smiled slightly, but held her breath. When she exhaled, her breath carried the words, "Six, maybe eight weeks." It was April; Brian died in June.

It was now a half-year later, and Pat couldn't wait to introduce me to Brenda Northrup. "She's a character," said Pat, laughing while shaking her head. She explained that the entire staff of Mission Hill had been trying to get Brenda to stop smoking, with limited and slightly ludicrous results. If Kevin had been feeble and Andy was nudging death, Brenda could hardly have been more alive. It could have been Auntie Mame who answered our knock on her door, "Okay, honey, come on in—come see Brenda!"

Brenda Northrup
and Pat Gibbons

33

Watching Pat while I loaded the camera and moved around the room, I realized that she gave to everyone the gift she gave to me. Pat gives herself. She was giving herself to Brenda—razor-thin, nearly bald, chain-smoking and grinning Brenda. When Pat is with you, you are the only person in her life. She doesn't study you, like a clinician; or analyze you, like a therapist; or measure you, like a journalist. She takes you in, like a long-lost friend who cannot get enough of hearing the news of your life.

Watching Pat with Brenda, I remembered the day she'd explained the signs of death to me, so I would know what was happening when Brian neared the end. I remembered her patience, but also her certainty.

When you set about dying, you start to close up your affairs and your world. You clean up what you can, forgive what you must, and settle accounts as best you're able. Then you narrow the circle of friends to people you want to be with. The one many of us have wanted at the center of that circle—the one I hope will be there for me—is Pat Gibbons.

**<u>Tina</u>**. Our divorce had not been pretty, and I wasn't sure how Brian's family would respond to my attempts at reconciliation. As he visited crises and hospitals with greater and greater frequency in 1992 and early 1993, I knew there was no time to

*March 9, 1994*

*Dear Mary,*

*My brother J. had AIDS, and I vowed I would not have any regrets when he died. I was given the gift of being one of his caregivers, driving to Minneapolis on weekends to be with him. The day he died, his partner of nine years, S., my mother and I sat with him. We were all able to be touching him while he took his last breath. I feel very glad we were able to be with him at the moment of his transformation into freedom.*

*J. wanted to be cremated and to have his ashes spread on the mountain top in Wyoming where we had hiked together. In the end, we buried half the ashes next to our dad who had died earlier in the year; this helped my mother's grief greatly. In August I went back to the Medicine Bow Mountains west of Laramie, Wyoming, and doing the last thing I could do for him, I spread the remaining ashes there. I will never forget that intimate moment. . . .*

*J. D.*
*Minnesota*

hesitate.

Brian's sister Tina knew the same thing. If she were going to care for Brian, she needed to give up her career in restaurant management and make him the focus of her life. So she did, becoming Brian's fulltime caregiver.

Most caregiving is done by family members. It's ordinary. But it is never common. And neither is Tina. Watching her with Brian I was awed by her stamina, her confidence, her love, and her humor. When he was excited, irrational, even mean, she was steady and gracious. When he would not let her out of his sight, she simply—cheerfully—settled in. And when, at the end, Brian and I wanted hours alone, she responded with joy, not jealousy.

Brian and Tina

Between Brian's death and writing this book, Tina moved into our home. She is family. And she is a caregiver extraordinaire.

**<u>Manny Souza, RN</u>**. When Brian grew very sick, and I came to spend time with him, Manny was there. He was, and remains, a person who thrives on being a caregiver. It isn't merely what he does; it's who he is.

"What do you say when you walk into the room of someone who's dying?" I asked him during our first meeting. " 'How are you?' doesn't seem quite right." He didn't laugh at me, or underscore my feelings of honest ignorance. He smiled and said, "Ask *what* they're feeling, not how. Ask what they think about what's happening to them. Ask, and then listen."

I've heard people discuss "burnout" at half the conferences I've keynoted. They explain that they have grown so weary of the dying that they can't go on.

Manny has never mentioned burning out. I'm not sure he thinks it's possible. He behaves as though he were called to be a caregiver, as if this is his only sure purpose on earth. He talks about caregiving as I've heard professional athletes talk about championship games, in terms reserved for life's experiences that transcend words.

What Manny may do best of all is listen. When he heard Brian's restlessness that final Sunday morning, he knew the end was near. When he heard me crying too long, he came to end my vigil. And when I asked him, though my grief and terror, "What do I do now, Manny?" he thought for a moment before he answered me. It was as if he wanted to be sure he had listened first.

Manny Souza, RN. Listener. Caregiver. Hero.

Manny Souza

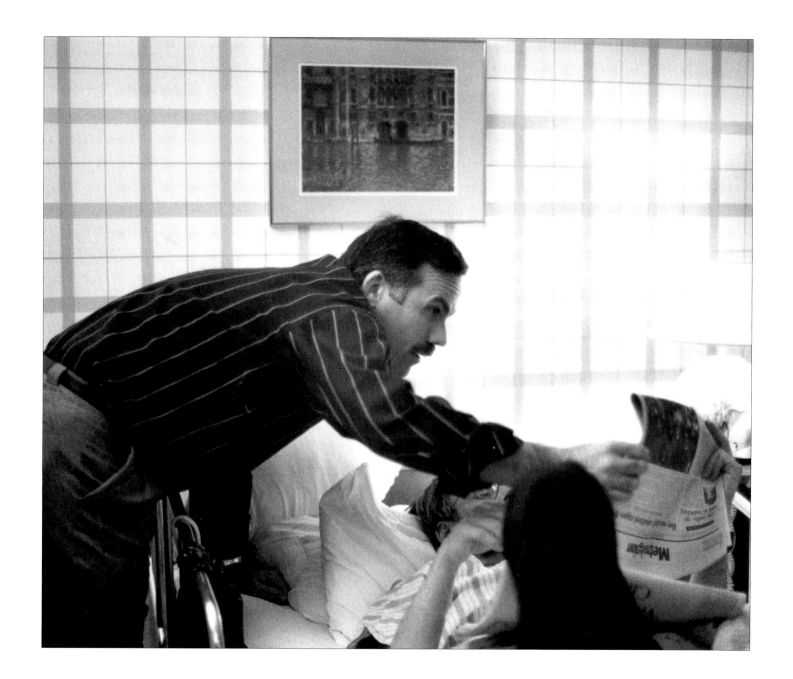

Scott and Robert at
Mission Hill Hospice

C.S. Lewis wrote, in the days following his wife's death, "I did not fear that God had ceased to exist. The greater fear was this: that I should turn toward God and say, 'So this is what you are really like.'"

If we cannot turn our faces away from death, then we must at least remember that death is not what God is really like. God is more like the laughter that follows our sweeter memories, the quiet breeze that once lifted his favorite kite, the sunshine that filtered through the leaves above Brian's hiding place in Boston Common. God is more like the canvas that Brian started and the boys finished, in colors that they loved.

Or, if you would like to know what God is really like, consider Manny Souza. In days of pain, his focus was comfort; in hours of distress and embarrassment, his only goals were peace and dignity. When Brian and I needed a night together, he was encouraging; when we needed a stronger hand, he was there before we had asked. When Brian was uncertain, Manny was convincing; when all we could do was weep, Manny hugged us with quiet joy.

And when his struggle was over, it was Manny who lifted me from Brian and said, when I asked what I could do next, "Now that you know, you must tell them what it's like."

We would do well as a company of pilgrims to look toward the likes of Manny Souza and whisper to God, "So, this is what you are really like."

*Excerpt from "Listening for Isaiah"*
*Remembrance by Mary Fisher*
*Brian Campbell Memorial Service*
*Provincetown, Massachusetts*
*Saturday, September 25, 1993*

# ATLANTA
## November 1993

AIDS and religion have had an uneasy relationship from the beginning of the epidemic. Sexually transmitted diseases prevalent among gay men do not constitute a typical Sunday School topic.

Some communities of faith have been faithless. They've judged and rejected those who most needed to hear about grace and comfort. It's an unusually brutal blow to those weakened by disease and terrorized by death. God deserves better from those who claim to be his children, and so do God's children with AIDS.

But judgmentalism and rejection are only part of the AIDS-and-religion legacy in America. Rabbis and priests have told hostile congregations that God asks for obedient service to "the lepers of our age." Pastors and laypeople have organized teams that brought food and love to people with AIDS while recruiting an army of caregivers for whom AIDS became a call of God.

Most Americans hate what's broken and can't be fixed; we have no patience for it, and we don't like hearing about it. But caregivers aren't

🦋 EXCERPT 🦋

*Growing up in a Jewish home near Detroit, I was encouraged by my parents to adopt lofty goals. Speaking in Christian congregations was not one of them.*

Excerpt from
"When Grief Meets Grace"
Sermon by Mary Fisher
Cascade United Methodist Church
Atlanta, Georgia
Sunday, November 21, 1993

Derrick and Donna Meyers
with Torinthia Stewart

40

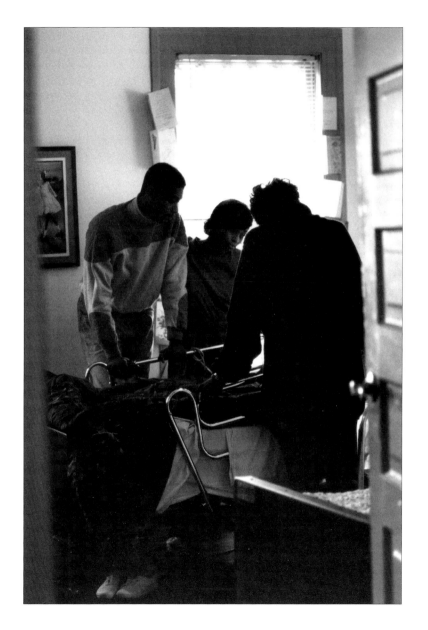

trying to fix something. They are helping us experience something, by loving us through hours of our lives in which what's broken isn't going to be fixed. They understand that life in the face of death is still life.

And faith, when found in a hospice, is still faith. It isn't cocksure or arrogant. Caregivers don't claim that faith has given them the answer to all life's questions. Rather, they think of faith as the gift that enables them to live, and to love, when there are no answers.

**The House that God Built**. "Haven House," says Metta G. Johnson, RN, BSN, OCN, and co-director of Nursing, "is a home of love and nursing care for ten patients with AIDS—a house that God built." She believes it. Only the foolhardy would challenge her by pointing out that God evidently used her to imagine, create, fund, and manage the facility before installing her as resident matriarch and caregiver.

I showed up on a chilly Saturday, bundled in coats and cameras. In the company of her husband and Haven House co-founder (and chief financial officer), Clyde, Metta made me feel at home within minutes.

"You need to meet Babsey," she said, leading me past a nurses' station in the broad hallway of the wonderfully refurbished old home. Babsey Meyers was already on the downside of fifty, one of those women who contracted AIDS before she knew heterosexual women could be infected. She perhaps had not thought it was possible. But it didn't matter, certainly not any more. All that mattered now was staying alive, and staying comfortable. Which is what her caregivers were intent on achieving: her sister, a powerful woman whose will and stamina matched the challenge of death and dying; her son, who regarded caring for his parent not as a duty but as a privilege; her daughter-in-law, Donna, who said, matter-of-factly, "This is what it means to be family."

David Camp took up residence in a room not far away. His mother, Alice, and one of Haven House's nurses were in the room when I pushed open the door to ask if I could come in.

David was momentarily alert, even cheerful, but he'd been "coming in and out" of consciousness, according to his mother. He was so excited that I was there he acted almost like a child being visited by a baseball star. I felt strange.

Alice adored David. If he were childlike again—welcoming the stuffed animal she'd brought today—she was happy to be motherly, to care for her child. When she sat in a nearby chair, and he smiled, she beamed. Her hands constantly smoothed the sheets. His slightest movement was her cue to act, and she knew what each movement meant,

*David Camp went peacefully on Thanksgiving evening [November 25, 1993]. Last Saturday, when you were with him, was the last day he was intelligible—except for Tuesday, when he made it very clear he was accepting and peaceful, and wanted everything stopped. . . .*

*Babsey died Saturday at 2:30 in the morning, peacefully, with all her family beside her.*

*I'm so grateful you were able to meet them.*

Personal Correspondence from
Metta G. Johnson
December 3, 1993

David and Alice Camp

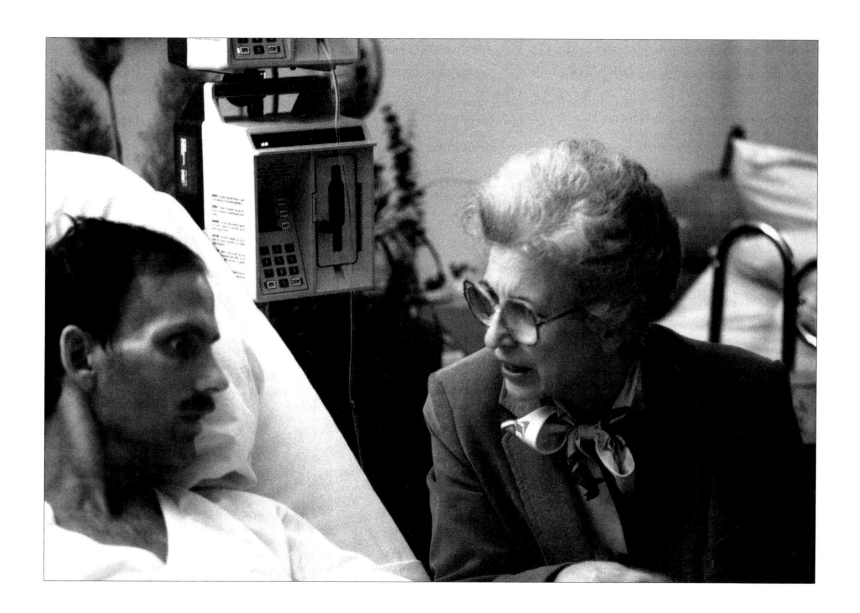

what he wanted. A shiver in his arm meant he wanted to be moved. A turn of the head meant he needed a drink. She was stoic without being cold, in charge without being overbearing, caring for her man-child as he slipped away. They took such joy in each other, such pride—she was his caregiver and he was her hero. They sparkled together.

I was leaving Haven House when the staff and a few residents called

me into a lounge-like area for a group photo. The place smelled of antiseptic and cooking and room spray. We were crowding around a table, joking and hugging, when I noticed two men together in a corner, one of them attached to IV tubes, covered with a blanket, and the other bending over him, talking softly. I was embarrassed at the noise we were making and went over to apologize.

Leonard Scott had been fighting AIDS for a long time and was so pleased that his friend of more than twenty years, Samuel Kemp, had come from

＊ CORRESPONDENCE ＊

*March 20, 1996*

*Dear Mary,*

*I've always wanted to be normal and not have to have everybody feeling bad for me. But I have a lot more health problems and it takes forever to explain.*

*It seems like you really believe in God. I wish I had faith and courage like you do. I want to be able to trust. I know that, with God, you don't have to worry about dying. That's very neat that God called you by your name, Mary. I wish he would do that to me.*

*L.F.*
*Michigan*

Leonard Scott with Samuel Kemp

Common Ground prayer circle

Los Angeles to spend the weekend with him.

"I was just in Los Angeles myself," I said to Samuel. "I preached there last Sunday at First AME Church. It was the most moving Sunday I've ever had. I'll tell you, the world's greatest caregivers sing in their choir. It was unbelievable."

"Yes," Samuel said with a nod. "Yes, I know. I stood right behind you last Sunday. I sing in that choir."

**Common Ground**. The Atlanta Interfaith AIDS Network runs a day-care center for persons with AIDS (and sponsored the candlelight Service of Hope and Healing at which I spoke). It was there I met Reverend Robert A. and Louise Hudak, co-directors and co-caregivers at Common Ground.

While visiting Common Ground I realized how easily we stereotype "homeless people." We don't talk about them as "people without houses." We don't think of them as "Jonathan" or "Abigail," "Mr. Pazarolli" or "Mrs. Van Dyke." They're "homeless people."

I said, during my remarks at the candlelight service, that "I am not a patient or a 'case' for anyone. I am not a victim, so I need no pity. I am merely an ordinary person with an ordinary name, Mary; like you, a common pilgrim stumbling along the way. . . ." As I was touring Common Ground, a man who someone pointed out to me as "homeless" came up and said, "Hi, Mary, I'm a pilgrim, too."

We were, literally, on common ground.

*❧ Excerpt ❧*

*Some of us have come tonight to grieve the loss of loved ones. We remember them with tears. We feel the aching lonesomeness that follows such loss. They are not numbers or statistics or victims to us. They are persons with names.*

*If I could, tonight, I would offer healing and a cure. I would promise health. I would laugh at the virus and invite you to join in the laughter. But the only healing I have to offer is prayer; the only cure, a family of people full of compassion. . . .*

*And for all, I have this promise*

**Project Open Hand**. Two meals a day were being prepared for and delivered to 750 homebound Atlantans, most of them people with AIDS. If you were homebound and needed to warm your food, but didn't have a microwave, they loaned you one. If you had a pet, they brought pet food. In other words, they cared.

Sometimes, a Project Open Hand brochure told me, these volunteers were the only human contact for those who received food: "Husbands, wives, lovers, and family members are often gone. Some have died of AIDS. Some are unable to help. Some are afraid to stay. So, we're providing more than food. We're offering Atlanta hope."

Most of the people I photographed here were older, many of them retired. As I shot pictures I asked, "Why do you do this?" A few pulled faces and made jokes ("What else is an old geezer to do?" drawled one laughing man). One said, "It's just fun to be together, like a club." And most echoed the idea summarized by a woman who said she was seventy-six: "Well, I don't want for anything, except I need to do something worth doing."

*by which we can hold on to a moment of comfort: God knows us by our names—He remembers us not only when we gather for prayer but also when, alone, we go to grieve. Those whom we've lost have not been lost by God. As surely as my children hear me calling—"Max! Zack!"—so surely have they heard their Father calling them by name.*

*Excerpt from "My Name Is Mary"*
*Address by Mary Fisher*
*Service of Hope and Healing for People*
*Living with HIV/AIDS*
*Atlanta, Georgia*
*Sunday, November 21, 1993*

Project Open Hand volunteer

The first human act of care-giving may well have been one person offering food to another. All these years later, it's something still worth doing.

Common Ground counselor and client

*We often think of grief as a brief stage of mourning. But living with HIV extends the duration of grief to the length of a lifetime. We live, infected, wondering what will give in first, and last; unsure what promise to make our children, or ourselves; wondering when the distant bell will suddenly toll more closely. We do not so much recover from this grief as learn to live with it.*

*Because the epidemic first surfaced in America's gay communities, this grief has been compounded. Old patterns of discrimination came to life with new brutality. Traditional sources of comfort—the home and the church—became, instead, tribunals of judgment. Parents rejected children. Voices rang out from pulpits saying the virus was God's idea, speculating that HIV was divine retribution. Intimate messages of rejection were matched by public policies of indifference.*

*For the AIDS community in America, the voice of God heard from communities of faith has been terribly muted. Temples should have raised high the roofbeams to bring them in; churches should have shouted messages of grace from the rooftops. But what most members of the AIDS family have heard is whispers about their morality and the hope that, like modern-day lepers, they will not get too close.*

*Excerpt from "When Grief Meets Grace"*
*Sermon by Mary Fisher*
*at Cascade United Methodist Church*
*Atlanta, Georgia*
*Sunday, November 21, 1993*

# RIKERS ISLAND

New York City Department of Correction
Rose M. Singer Center for Women

## December 1993

Prisoners of war who come home alive often talk little of the torture they endured and much about the ingenious means used by fellow prisoners to care for one another. You cannot wall out compassion.

I was not sure what I'd find at Rikers Island, but I'd been told that several amazing women were caregivers to the inmates. In a setting where so many women had histories of abuse and addictions, and high-risk behaviors of almost every kind, it was inevitable that they would come to prison bringing AIDS with them. Perhaps it was equally inevitable that, once there, they would find caregivers: chaplains, educators, social workers, even matrons and guards. I was amazed by the compassion they demonstrated in the least compassionate of all surroundings.

But most of the caregivers for women with AIDS in prison were other women in prison. There were dozens of them at Rikers Island. When women stood to hesitantly admit that they, too, had tested positive for the AIDS virus, the response from their fellow inmates was

❧ CORRESPONDENCE ❧

*Through his willingness to take risks, to "stand up" and disclose his own HIV-positive status, Louis Jones has done what I've never seen anyone else do: He has, literally, created a community in which others who are called "homeless" have found their way "home."*

*Personal Correspondence*
*Charles Eaton, Director*
*City of New York*
*Department of Health*
*February 9, 1994*

Rev. Fredelia Christof and Rev.
Maria Lopez with Sandra Ocasio
and Mercedes Cruz

potent. In spite of prison-culture toughness, they wept together, holding one another and rocking back and forth, reassuring each other like the mothers and grandmothers who held them years before.

Victor Frankl once said that he and his fellow survivors of the Nazi death camps would always keep alive the memories of extraordinary heroes who had been imprisoned with them. The most remarkable, he said, were the men who walked through the camps giving away their last piece of bread so others could live another day.

Compassion has limits, but surely it is not bound by walls.

**The Prison.** Captain Cooper, a woman of impressive dimensions, could play a penitentiary matron in one of those 1950s, black-and-white B movies that haunt television at three in the morning. When you see her, you know you want to be good. But when I spoke at Rikers' afternoon program, telling my own life story and inviting others to share theirs, it was Captain Cooper who kept the guards from ending the meeting before inmates worked up the courage to tell their stories.

One woman stood to say, "I got tested today." She didn't have the results yet, but she was sure she had the virus. Her story chilled the room.

A woman popular among the inmates surprised everyone by saying, "I've never told anyone here, but. . .I have AIDS." It took courage to say it. And when she talked about her fears—the loss of her chil-

*February 3, 1996*

*Dear Mary,*

*I am yet another face of AIDS, another mother who one day will have to leave her child, another person who is trying earnestly to make a difference in a world where she sees so much more to do. I am a registered nurse. My family and I are statistics, but like everyone else we are a lesson to be learned, fighting to show that this illness is a viral warrior, not a moral failing.*

*While I fight with my own AIDS, there is a greater battle to be waged against the paralyzing fear and panic in the medical community. People with AIDS are made to suffer shame, humiliation and embarrassment in a system where people have taken an ethical oath to respect dignity and well-being. Until this is changed, prejudice will breed on hospitals' healing grounds. . . .*

*L.A.*
*Pennsylvania*

HIV inmate with HIV baby

dren, the anger of her husband—her courage blended with tears, hers and those of many others in the room.

Two women came up to me (the guards let them get close enough to whisper) and told me, "I'm positive, too."

I visited the nursery area where mothers with AIDS, and their babies (some infected), are living among other mothers and other infants. To prevent discrimination, I was told, no one knew which mothers and which babies had AIDS. But it was a futile attempt at distinction. Two women had died of AIDS days before I arrived; their condition had been no secret, and the cause of their death was no surprise.

I was packing my camera equipment when a prison worker came into the small room where I was working. She closed the door and cleared her throat. I knew she was going to tell me

I wouldn't be able to use my film. I had already taken a deep breath and prepared my argument when she said, "You won't believe this, I suppose, but I have AIDS, too. I've told only one person here, before you." We talked for a few minutes, and hugged.

**The Reverend**. The Reverend Fredelia Kristof is Executive Director of the Samaritan Women's Prison Project at Rikers. She is undaunted by the challenges of a ministry behind bars. So is the Reverend Maria Lopez, the prison's chaplain.

I asked Maria, "Don't you ever just want to give up?" She told me the story of a shepherd who had a hundred sheep. "Ninety-nine of them were safe in the fold, but one wandered off," she said. "Now what would a good shepherd do?" I supposed a good shepherd would go find the lost sheep.

"Um-hm," she hummed, "that's right. You know, I was just following that Good Shepherd, and these are the sheep I found."

Some people would think of Reverend Kristof or Reverend Lopez as prisoners of their own ministry, inmates among inmates. But they wouldn't, nor would I. They are caregivers among caregivers.

Rev. Fredelia Christof and
Rev. Maria Lopez

*Three months ago I came to Rikers Island for the first time. I came then as a photographer, planning to take away a series of pictures. But I left as a woman, carrying with me . . .some of the strength and courage that I found here. From the woman who told me that she, too, has AIDS, I took the certainty that I am not alone, that there are others who understand the fear of losing our children and our lives. From the woman who spoke of years in addiction, and now months in recovery, I took the strength to maintain my own recovery. From the woman who hugged me long and hard, and whispered that she would pray for me, I took the hope by which to live "on the outside" for another ninety days.*

*. . .And now I've come back as one of you: a woman who knows the taste of terror as well as the promise of hope; a woman articulate about her failings and hard-pressed to name a single achievement; a woman in whom good intentions flower, only to wilt when I grow weary. I've come back not to praise you, nor even to challenge you, but to congratulate you, and to thank you for caring for me.*

*Excerpt from "When We Grow Weary"*
*Commencement Address by Mary Fisher*
*STEP Program*
*Rikers Island, New York*
*Friday, March 11, 1994*

Mercedes Cruz and Sandra Ocasio

# WEST PALM BEACH

## January 1994

When I was pregnant with my first child, Max, I led classes and groups at Gratitude House, a small extended-treatment center for alcoholic and addicted women in West Palm Beach, Florida. Work at Gratitude House was a step toward my own full recovery, a response to Betty Ford's admonition that we should each become "rocks that we toss into the ponds of our own communities, sending out ripples of service." Gratitude House was my pond.

Two other programs are affiliated with Gratitude House: Connor's Nursery, where infants are placed while mothers stay at Gratitude House, and The Children's Place, a home for older, often abused youngsters.

After I'd learned my own diagnosis, I would take Max and, by then, his little brother Zack to Connor's Nursery. We brought toys. I'd watch Max toddle around and enjoy friends with whom he'd make messes while Zack napped in his stroller. I wanted Max and Zack to have friends whose families had been infected with AIDS the way ours had been.

It was too early for my sons, of course. The lesson never registered

Jenny Cray at
Connor's Nursery

58

with them. But I learned something. When I went back to take photographs, I realized that AIDS had taken Brian, and my children were one parent removed from an orphanage.

**<u>Choosing Love</u>**. Some of the children at Connor's are born with AIDS. Some have a crack or heroin or cocaine addiction at birth. Some are transferred from the hospital, some brought in by hopeless mothers, some simply abandoned.

The children are, in every sense of the word, "the community's babies." They belong to us. They are the consequence of our values and policies, the children who pay the cost of our indifference. They are, while they live, if they live, living indictments. Seeing them, we should feel less pity and more guilt.

Then come caregivers: grandfathers and grandmothers, women and men—single and married—high school students and college interns. They're tentative at first, wondering if a child with AIDS is too feeble to be lifted and fed, patted and put down to nap. But with time, they grow comfortable. And with more time, they grow attached.

There are heartwarming scenes here. Children smiling in response to tickles and hugs. Laughter floating over the playroom. Infants with eyes too heavy to stay awake, tucking into the shoulder of a caregiver.

*I've found other places with other names and a mission as compelling as Connor's, with needs as burning as yours, met by people as devoted as you. You are unique. But you are not alone. And that's a reason for great hope in my life.*

*Recent news reports of [life-prolonging drugs for people with AIDS] have brought both good news and bad. The good news is that, for some, life will extend longer. But with every scientific advance that prolongs the lives of some people with AIDS, the need to care for those with AIDS grows greater. No one, least of all me, hopes that those with AIDS die quickly; we've seen too much of the dying already. But the alternative, since we've not yet slowed the infections, is an American AIDS community that grows larger every ten minutes.*

*The AIDS community does not place its hope in the hands of those who create drugs; we place it in the hands of those who create community. Therefore, you must stay the course. The epidemic has not ended, nor has the need for your work, or time, or contributions, or caregiving. If anything, the need is greater than ever.*

*Excerpt from "Coming Home to Connor's"*
*Address by Mary Fisher*
*"Catch a Rising Star" Gala*
*West Palm Beach, Florida*
*Thursday, January 30, 1997*

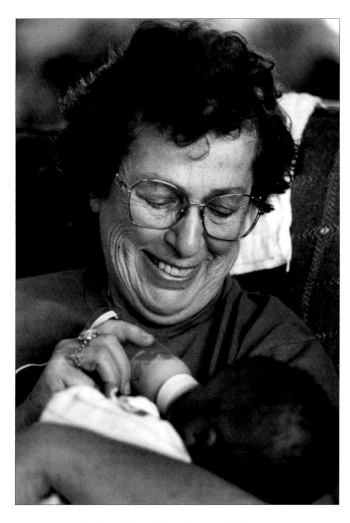

Barbara Harnick at Connor's Nursery

But it's not all lullabies and sweetness. When sixty-two year-old Johnie Mae Frazier cradled her grandson with AIDS and broke into "Swing Low, Sweet Chariot," it was a real possibility that she sang about in the second stanza:

If you get there before I do,
Comin' for to carry me home,
Tell all'a my friends that I'm comin' too,
Comin' for to carry me home.

Nothing in life, I'm told by those who know, is as hard as losing a child. And every caregiver at Connor's who loves a child with AIDS is setting out, consciously, to endure that pain. The illness isn't a surprising discovery made against their own will, like that heard by parents whose children go from robust health to, say, leukemia's fevers. Caregivers here know, from the moment they lift the first child to their breast, where the road will lead.

And, one after another, time after time, they choose to love.

In the years since last I visited many of you, I've come to realize that places like Connor's were classrooms in my life, and many of you have been my teachers.

I came here first as many of you did, to help. I thought I was here because I had something to offer. But what happened to me here was that, in helping in little ways, I became a learner.

I learned here that bad things happen in life through no particular evil of our own. At Gratitude House we see that a mother can fall into addiction, and a child into abuse, without either having ever intended it. In our own lives, we become what we'd never imagined being: a pilgrim on the road to AIDS. Bad things happen, and we will need comfort.

But I also learned here what's required for a community to respond to the needs of those within it. The lesson was so simple that I nearly missed it: All we have to do is have each of us do what we do best. Mothers who are gifted at mothering need to do what they do best: mother. What's needed is not for grandfathers to become something other than they are, but for them to be exactly what they are: grandfathers. Lonesome widows can come here to know that their life's meaning has not passed with their life's partner. Those who are single, or childless, or wanting to wipe a child's tears or feel the warmth of her hug—come here, and be human.

*Excerpt from*
*"Coming Home to Connor's"*
*Address by Mary Fisher*
*"Catch a Rising Star" Gala*
*West Palm Beach, Florida*
*Thursday, January 30, 1997*

Volunteer at Connor's Nursery

# NEW YORK CITY
## January 1994

Epidemics tend to spread downward in society, away from power and toward those who are most vulnerable.

Power, wealth, and health tend to travel together. Power often yields to, or rises from, wealth; with wealth one usually finds better diet, safer neighborhoods, more education, and substantially improved healthcare. If we can afford it, we generally live longer.

But America's most vulnerable populations are those without the protection of the power or wealth that equip us for good health. They need to find security elsewhere: in relationships that can turn abusive, in alcohol and other drugs that offer a moment of respite, in low-paying jobs reserved for those on a fast track to nowhere. Those populations are most vulnerable when they are minorities among disinterested majorities (think of African-Americans and Hispanics), or when they are distrusted and sometimes despised (think of gays and lesbians or Haitian "boat people").

It isn't impossible for recovering alcoholics, or unwanted refugees, or released prisoners to finish their educations, start their careers, and

Phyllis Anderson and Jecenia DeJesus

build security in themselves and for their futures. It's just very, very difficult.

Before the illness was named AIDS (auto-immune deficiency syndrome), it was called GRID. The "G" stood for Gay. Gay people still get AIDS. But every year the percentage of those being infected climbs among youth (half of those infected last year were under twenty-five), women (rates of infection are climbing, and our rates of death are already highest), and people of color, especially African-Americans and Hispanics.

A population is truly vulnerable when society as a whole—the so-called "majority"—believes that population is disposable. Field slaves with broken backs were short-lived. So were German Jews in 1937. So are women with AIDS and no financial means, in America, today.

**<u>STANDUP Harlem</u>**. The incredible Louis Jones has a vision of people caring for themselves and for each other. He calls his program STANDUP Harlem. And he has AIDS. But what matters here isn't whether you do or do not have AIDS. What matters is that you care for yourself and for others. In neighborhoods where crack houses dominate, STANDUP Harlem is a safe house. It's a place where people without family come to create family together.

Louis Jones was amused by all the camera equipment I brought with me. "You don't need that much stuff," he said quietly. "We aren't that big a deal."

Louis Jones

He was modest. He kept sliding out of range when I would raise the camera, not wanting to be the center of attention. He nudged me toward Phyllis Anderson, a graduate of the Rikers Island STEP Program and now a counselor and caregiver at STANDUP Harlem. "Talk to her," he said. "Take pictures of Phyllis." I did. And while I shot film, she explained the program in intensely personal terms:

> I've watched a lot of my friends die, and nobody said "Why?" They just died. My best friend died. A first cousin. A stepsister. We still didn't talk about it, didn't ask, "Why's this happening?" Now I'm positive and, you know, I'm vocal.
>
> When I was in jail, I had so much AIDS literature and brochures stuck under my mattress that it was, like, up to here, you know?—all lumpy. And I read that stuff. Because when I got my diagnosis, I was incarcerated, and the

first thing that came to my mind was, in a year, I'm going to be dead. And then I found out you don't have to die. You can live with this. I can speak only for myself, but being positive has been a blessing to me.

I always wanted to do something different but I always said, "Oh, man, I'm too old and I don't want to go back to school. By the time I get out, who's going to hire me anyhow? I'll be real, real old." And, you know, I did it. I went back. I learned, became a bookkeeper. And now I've got a job in human services. I'm a caregiver.

People were coming and going. Men, women, some with children. Groups were forming into circles for meetings (Alcoholics Anonymous at one end of the living room, Narcotics Anonymous upstairs). Everywhere people were greeting each other with hugs.

Louis was standing near the kitchen, frowning, his hands draped over the shoulders of a slightly smaller man whose face was only inches from Louis'. Louis was talking softly, earnestly. The man could do nothing but listen.

Teenage mothers came through the door to care for each other and each other's children. Men without homes were settling in to be responsible fathers and friends. A daughter who had buried her mother, and her brother, and two children of her own, was making coffee. What united them was not AIDS—I couldn't tell who was positive, who wasn't—but the commitment against all the odds to convert strangers into family members. The insistence that "we will be family for each other" was

Dorothy and Theresa Poindexter

thick and tangible.

Phyllis introduced me to Jessie DeCenia. Jessie introduced me to the members of a peer group: Jecenia DeJesus, Larry Wharton, Melissa Jackson. They introduced me to Theresa Poindexter. I shot pictures. I asked questions. I listened.

"My mother died of AIDS on my nineteenth birthday." Jessie was talking. "September 7, 1991. I didn't know my mom had AIDS. I had no physical contact with my mother for nine or ten years, 'til just before she died. We were all raised in foster homes, group homes, you know." I didn't know, but I nodded. Jessie continued:

> That last year before she died, I remember sitting in my dorm room in school and I get this call. It's my mother. To this day, God knows how she got my number. It's, like, maybe ten months before she dies, and we're just talking over the phone. Except I've got this ten years of anger inside of me. She wants me to come over and see her, and I wasn't about to go see this woman. I didn't care what she was doing, you know?
>
> The day before she died, I was supposed to go visit her in the hospital—somebody said she was in the hospital. But I'm thinking, "I'm too depressed already." And that was my attitude, you know? Let her die, you know? Whatever. So she died. On my birthday.

Jessie talked. I shot pictures.(Click) She kept describing anger at a vagrant mother, without raising her voice, without gritting her teeth. (Click) It was just how things were. And now she was the mother-fig-

Larry Wharton, Jecenia DeJesus, and Melissa Jackson

ure. (Click) She left college and came back to get her little brother and a sister out of foster care, and to become family for them:

> I have an eleven-year-old at home. I see this little girl. . .this little girl who can talk to you about her mom who died of AIDS. And "this is how you get it" and "this is how you don't" and all about sex and everything. Eleven. My sister does this. She talks about her mother's status with AIDS and isn't even ashamed. It's just a fact. It's just what happened. And she doesn't even know my status.

Click.

> I was sitting in a group of girls yesterday, most of them positive, and young, you know, thirteen, fourteen, fifteen. Somebody said, "Hey, what do we need most?" And one girl gets up and says, "You know, sometimes I can—you know, I can deal with the AIDS and all. But sometimes I just feel like running home and telling my family, 'No, it was a mistake. I got cancer.' I want to say that." And she goes, "I wish I could just deal with the chemotherapy and, you know, stuff with cancer." And she goes, "It'd be a lot easier, you know." And then she starts crying, and talking about the stigma and the stereotypes, and being shunned. Because she misses her mother, you know? And her mother doesn't want her, you know, 'cause she has AIDS.

**Iris House**. I went from STANDUP Harlem to Iris House to interview people there. I met Marie Saint Cyr, the executive director. I met Linda Gang and Carolyn Finken and admired their caregiving. Everyone

Linda Gang and Marie
Saint Cyr, Iris House

at Iris House was kind and I took pictures and I went home. But I had not yet left Jessie, or Phyllis, or others who streamed through STANDUP Harlem. I did not do justice to Iris House. I was too overwhelmed by the fact that, maybe in both places, you couldn't distinguish between those who had AIDS and those who didn't.

The only distinction that really mattered was who was strong enough to care for someone else—physically, emotionally, spiritually—and who was not.

I was shooting photos at an AIDS housing program called STANDUP Harlem a month or two ago. A group of young, HIV-positive women were talking about their families and the rejection they felt. . . .

And I wondered if there is a moral difference between one virus and another. Why would we stiff-arm a daughter with AIDS while cuddling a daughter with cancer? I fear the answer is this: despite our loud rejections of fundamentalist TV screamers, we hold their beliefs, only more quietly. We think of AIDS as something earned, as if those who carry the virus made a wasting death their goal and must now go on to achieve it.

This is an ugly notion, as old as the Book of Job, the idea that when life is sleek and easy we're rolling around in blessings, and when life grows grim and hard the blessings are no longer there.

*Excerpt from "Speak Ye Comfortably to Jerusalem"*
*Address by Mary Fisher Temple Sinai*
*Pittsburgh, Pennsylvania*
*Sunday, April 24, 1994*

G·A·L·L·E·R·Y  O·F
C·A·R·E·G·I·V·E·R·S

Louise Hudak heals with hugs

Their brother, Troy, went to "another world"

Baseball's Giants, moral giants

. . . so full of life—Connor's volunteer, Helga Hargreaves

Steve, Rock and Abbey

Feeding the hungry in San Francisco

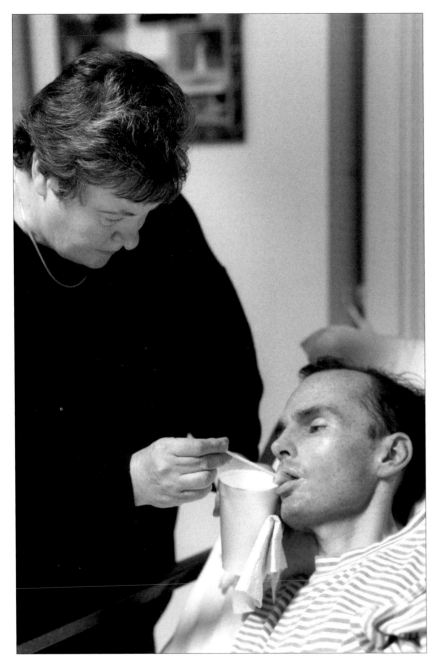

Some moms are there to the end

Playing at Rue's House, Los Angeles

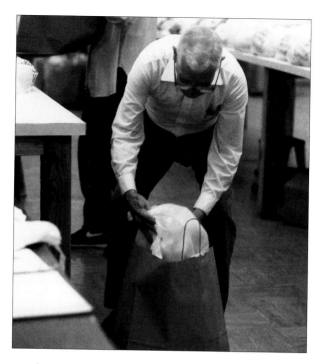

Filling a bag with
love in Atlanta

Stewart McKinney Hospice

Joy Page Cooke, Tim
Page—sister and
brother—always

Caregiving at any age

Remembering Chris—Chris
Brownlie Hospice L.A.
(photos right and below)

Sonia Gregerson feeding
Dominique at Connor's

When Bets Bostick touched Jeffrey Burchette
I felt love as well—Beacon Place, Greensboro

Tuesday's Child—Los Angeles

# Some of My Caregivers

I love being a mom!

Tina, Sister-in-law
extraordinaire

Beth and Jim

Zack and Max

# Some of My Caregivers

Mom and Dad

Max and Zack

Joy Prouty and Zack

Jim Heynen, Joy Prouty, Phillip Fisher, me and Brian Weiss

# KANSAS CITY

June 1994

Playwright Paul Rudnick once explained in *The New York Times* why gay writers have written comedies about AIDS. "Only money, rage, and science can conquer AIDS," he said. "But only laughter can make the nightmare bearable."

R. Ellen King is tall, white, short-haired, young or ageless (depending on the angle of the light), and beautiful. She is a social worker at SAVE Home in Kansas City, Missouri. She's had a bout with cancer. She's a caregiver. And she makes the nightmare bearable with, among other things, humor.

For all the wretched illnesses, and all the difficulties that attach to living on the edge of dying, caregiving is not entirely a somber or humorless process. Hospices are not as quiet as you might imagine if you've never visited one. Residences for people with AIDS are as likely as not to have children dashing through the hallways and tricycles crashing into walls. You walk through a door and smell food cooking. You hear phones ringing and pots clanging and glasses clinking together as tables are set and chairs are moved and people go about the daily rou-

Shawn, Emma, and
Rodney Wells

tine of living. And over the sound of all of it, more often than not, you hear people laughing. Telling jokes. Remembering the most ridiculous moments of their lives.

Some of the funniest hours I've spent, anywhere during my lifetime, have been spent with caregivers. And I mean funny, not just amusing. I'm not talking about slight smiles or quiet chuckles. I'm talking side-splitting, tummy-grabbing, laugh-till-you-cry, try-not-to-wet-your-pants group guffaws in settings most people avoid because they're afraid of them.

True caregiving is never a job, even when people are paid for it. It is always a joy. That's the source of both its mystery, and the hilarity.

**<u>SAVE Home</u>**. My visit had a ring of unreality about it. I was in Kansas City to help raise awareness and funds, so the media were an important part of the trip. Reporters—most of them good people doing a good job—were with me at the airport when I landed, at Saint Paul's Episcopal Church where I gave a noontime speech to pastors and lay leaders, at the gala "Ribbon of Hope Awards Dinner" and, in between, at my visit to SAVE Home. I had an entourage as well as a camera, and the former threatened to make the latter useless.

But I was rescued by Ellen King. She kept our pace lively. She found a way to occupy everyone else's attention for a little while so I could be alone with Emma J. Wells, a mother with a fierce sense of pride and a rollicking sense of joy.

Marsha Heffestad and David McKinney

Ellen told me about a client who was dying of AIDS. "This person said to me, 'You know, Ellen,'"—she always quotes people talking to her—"'there is something a lot worse than having AIDS in your life, and that's having AIDS and not having God in your life.'" For Ellen, giving care to those who need it is a spiritual experience. "Being with these people is the best prayer I can offer."

But when she tells the stories, they aren't usually religious. They're joyful, punctuated with funny twists and surprising endings.

"Did you know Elizabeth Taylor visited us a while ago?" she asked. I didn't know, but I was impressed. "The TV stations sent out people to get it all on video. After Miss Taylor left, she sent back some fast food and everybody was sitting around eating it. A reporter got a camera up close to one of our clients, who agreed to be on TV because he had something he wanted to say. So the reporter asks, 'What do you think about Miss Taylor's food?' and the resident says, without looking up, 'Did you know that I found out I was HIV-positive the same day my brother died of AIDS?' Then he looked straight into the camera, smiled, and said, 'And the hamburgers were great.'"

It's the rise and fall of life that makes for humor and for grief. Emma Wells knows all about it. She was clear in her conversation with me: She had AIDS and she had children (Rodney was then six, Shana was four), and she was committed not to let the disease make her incompetent to be her children's caregiver—even if she needed caregivers to help her be a caregiver.

*I believe that the nation's most substantial hope in our fight against AIDS rests within our religious, not our scientific, communities. If we must wait for science, I and millions of others, are doomed.*

*Scientific research is subject to policy and funding priorities, neither of which currently favors a search for either cures or preventatives for AIDS. In the face of budget cuts and tax revolts, there will not be enough political resolve to fuel the research needed to, among other things, save my life. I do not like this, but when I review national priorities, I know it.*

*. . .When I look back into American history and see the crisis of slavery, I notice that slavery was not revoked by scientists who studied genes and chromosomes and finally concluded that all human beings were alike. The force by*

*which the institution of slavery was ended was religious conversion, not laboratory discovery. If once religion had been used to defend slavery, over the course of time it also became the instrument by which slavery was destroyed.*

*A century later the civil rights movement was conceived in prayer and born in the basements of churches; it only spilled over into the streets when Rosa Parks decided to sit in the front of a bus.*

*. . .It is history, not desperation, that turns me with hope toward America's religious communities.*

*Excerpt from "Conversation with Mary Fisher"*
*Address by Mary Fisher*
*Ecumenical Fellowship at St. Paul's Episcopal Church*
*Kansas City, Missouri*
*Thursday, June 16, 1994*

Keith Smith and R. Ellen King

Caregivers giving care to caregivers. It made perfect sense.

And so did Emma's response to the somewhat insensitive question posed by a reporter who trailed me into her room: "Emma, do you ever think about leaving your children?" Name an honest mother who wouldn't have answered as Emma did—not out of grief at her AIDS, but out of honesty about her weariness—"Every second of every day."

We laughed and I took pictures.

"We had a very special client," Ellen told me not too long ago. "He taught children with mental impairments. He was an extraordinary teacher, because he was an extraordinary person.

"Children pick up stereotypes," she said, "and it happened to him. He was working his way around the classroom, trying to give each child personal attention despite all the noise and chaos, when one of his

Shawn Wells, Keith Smith, Rodney and Emma Wells, and Steven Long

kids called out, 'Hey you, fag!' He wheeled around and shot back, 'That's Mr. Faggot to you.'" She leaned back and laughed at the memory.

"We told that story at his memorial. It was so close to the essence of his character. So close."

*We are responsible for the moral character of our homes, our businesses, our communities. Our community's moral fabric does not just happen; we make it happen. We weave it from our own attitudes and behaviors. We define who will be praised and who will be shunted to the side, who will be lauded in the social pages of the* Kansas City Star *and who will be mocked in our private jokes. We decide who is desired and touchable, and who the untouchables will be, in our society.*

*Those with AIDS have, in community after community, become the untouchables. They've been isolated and despised. I've held weeping children who dared not tell anyone of their own diagnosis. I've listened to parents describe suffering their children endured at the hands not of the virus but of the neighbors. . . .*

*How do we account for this? Why would someone with a virus expect to be marked for prejudice and treated to abuse? Why would they fear? The answer, I'm afraid, is simple. They have seen us and our communities at work. They've seen that we treat AIDS not as a virus, but as a moral failure. We do not, really, believe that AIDS is like the flu and the common cold, striking both bishops and thieves without evidence of either innocence or guilt.*

*Excerpt from "Making Love an Option"*
*Address by Mary Fisher*
*Ribbon of Hope Awards Dinner*
*Kansas City, Missouri*
*Thursday, June 16, 1994*

# SAN FRANCISCO
## July and August 1994

The call had come some time earlier from the San Francisco Giants baseball team. Peter Magowan, managing partner of the team, wondered if I would be willing to speak briefly at the ball-park before the game on Saturday, July 31. It was going to be the Giants' "Until There's a Cure Day."

I described it later in the book *I'll Not Go Quietly*, where I recalled the ceremony and pageantry, the music and 50,000 fans roaring their solidarity with compassion. "Of all the wonderful things about that day," I wrote, "none was more wonderful than this: the Giants, for one whole day, made it okay to have AIDS. The sickness weakens you and the dying nearly breaks you. But for one warm, magical day in the ballpark by the bay, no one with AIDS was made to feel unworthy."

Peter Magowan, his wife Debbie, his colleagues—executive staff like Bob Rose, manager Dusty Baker, players and their wives (led by Rod and Stacey Beck)—are, collectively, caregivers for a community.

When Dr. Arie Brouwer left his post as General Secretary for the National Council of Churches to fight cancer, and eventually to lose the

Project Open Hand volunteers

fight, he kept a journal. On June 28, 1993, he wrote several remembrances of Dr. Martin Luther King's preaching. King's audiences, he noted, generally were made up not of princes and prime ministers but of people struggling to buy food, to care for their children, to endure life's injustices. "Thinking about that the other day," wrote Brouwer, "I was struck that King's focus was not on the enemy, not on the dogs, the bullwhips, the firehoses, the white hoods, or even on those who used these instruments of oppression. His focus was on what lay beyond the struggle, on 'the beloved community.' "

The San Francisco Giants, who play baseball in a city at the epicenter of the American AIDS epidemic, are choosing not to ignore the epidemic but to fight it. In doing so, they embody "the beloved community" that is public caregiving at its finest.

**Project Open Hand**. David Kennerly was the White House photographer during the Ford years, when I served in the President's advance office. We became friends. When David learned that I was going to San Francisco, and we discussed my photography of caregivers, he agreed to accompany me "to give a few pointers." Since he's won nearly every award there is to win for photojournalism, I was happy for his company and his advice.

Together, we toured Project Open Hand, San Francisco's premier food home-delivery program for persons with AIDS, hosted by Lynn Luckow, head of Jossey-Bass Publishing in San Francisco and then the

✦ EXCERPT ✦

*I congratulate Project Open Hand for a record of devoted service to those of us who are pilgrims on the road to AIDS. For those who grow hungry on this road, you provide food. For those who are lonely, you become family. For those who give up hope, you offer reason to stay another day and walk another mile. Some of you are, like me, HIV-positive; some of you are not. For the moment, it is the condition of your soul, not of your blood, that matters most. You are heroes along the road to AIDS.*

*Excerpt from "Remarks at
Project Open Hand"
Address by Mary Fisher
San Francisco, California
Monday, August 1, 1994*

Project Open Hand volunteers

newly-elected president of Project Open Hand's board. He was justifiably proud of the program which had become the prototype for meal-delivery programs and food banks across the nation.

I intended only to take pictures, but when we arrived, it was a media event of sorts. A new chief of staff, Tom Nolan, had been appointed by the board and was being introduced to the staff and community. I gave a speech. The staff stopped work to listen, leaving us with nothing to photograph.

Eventually the formalities ended and the media left. David and I donned aprons and white hats and helped prepare food. Still wearing cooks' outfits, we finally pulled out cameras and got a few shots of the remarkable people who do remarkable things for people with AIDS.

February 21, 1997

*Dear Mary,*

*I am a mother and a grandmother, and my daughter and grandson are HIV-positive. It's been seven months since we learned of their infection. I love them to pieces. . . .*

*I felt that I needed to seek support, and what better place to seek it than the house of the Lord, the church I have attended for more years than I can recall, where I taught children and youth in Sunday School. I felt that these people would love me through the toughest trial to be visited upon me.*

*But reality struck hard in this community of brothers and sisters, and they have more or less closed their hearts, minds and doors to me and my family. It is so lonely here that sometimes I feel as though the world has closed me out and there is no one to help me back.*

*Does it ever get easier?*

D.F.
*Maryland*

Micaela Salort, George Simmons, Charlie Garfield, Douglas Clark, Eric Poche, Carlo Pinna, and Ronnie Ashley at Shanti Hospice

## Project Open Hand Food Bank.

I was tired. It had been three days without breaks, early mornings to late nights, media and events and the boys. I didn't want to make a second stop. And I didn't want to offend the good people who invited us. But I was tired. Even the photos I took at the food bank are tired. I look at them, and I remember: tired.

Maybe the people who work at the food bank feel the same way some days. When they do, they also show up, tired. Because they're caregivers.

## Shanti Hospice.

People who know AIDS in San Francisco know Dr. Charlie Garfield, who has, among other things, authored a book on caregiving. It was Charlie who met us at the door, and Charlie who guided me into a conference room so I could take pictures of staff members. We met as a group to talk: Charlie, George Simmons, Eric Poche, Ronnie Ashley, Carlo Pinna, Micaela Salort, Douglas Clark, and a few others who drifted in and out of the conversation. Near the end of our time, my sons joined us. (They connected immediately with Carlo, and I love the photograph of them together. *See p. 15*)

Our conversation was all about caregiving. Micaela Salort, director of the hospice, wondered how Ronnie Ashley could keep managing a camping experience for children with AIDS year after year. "How do you do this for the long haul? I mean, Ronnie, how do you go to the camp and have three kids die and a counselor die in the middle of camp? How do we stop to remember the dead and still keep on giving energy to the living?"

George Foster, a volunteer hospice caregiver for more than ten years, thought the answer was found in "knowing that we're not any different, any of us—not those who give care or those who need it. We share humanness. We share common values and ideas and feelings. We get bonded."

Micaela Salort and Carlo Pinna

They also share a common frustration: bureaucracies and "professionalism." They are angry at systems that purport to give care but are more concerned about regulations than compassion. Charlie pointed to the difference between "the heart of the caregiving, folks like you," and "the administrative overlay." George railed against those for whom "caregiving has become a business, a several-billion-dollars-a-year business" in which client deaths are "reported on voicemail." They remembered their ex-colleague who became an ex-client, and who had died a week after he explained, as a member of a public panel, what it means

Ronnie Ashley and Charlie Garfield

to work in the AIDS community: "It means to love," he had said.

That memory triggered others. "How do we deal with the multiple deaths?" asked Micaela. "One by one, they're tough. But when they accumulate, dozens and then hundreds, year after year—what do we do with all that?"

We were all silent for a moment, and then Ronnie told us a story from his Native American heritage:

Our people have a tradition. When they have a piece of clay that must be molded into a very fine pot, they do it. They knead the clay, and shape it, and fire it. And then they break it. They pound the broken pieces back down to dust, and they add that to new clay. They make another pot, and they fire it. And they break it again, and do it all over again. Over and over they make the pot, they fire the pot, they break the pot, until they make the final, perfect pot.

Everyone we've lost has a name. We remember them, even though they have been broken by death. It's our memories of them, the things they taught us and left for us to do, that harden our clay, making us more perfect and stronger to do what must be done.

When the cameras go off and the celebrations take a recess, your work is not all glitter and glory. Kitchens can get hot and tempers can grow short. Some of us with whom you work are sick, some are depressed, some are dying. It is not always easy for us to be grateful, or for you to be patient with our ingratitude. And so the days grow long and sometimes hard.

Some of us show up for news conferences; such contributions may be important. But you show up for work, and that is how you've earned the rank of hero. Day after day, when it's inconvenient, you've set aside other priorities to feed the hungry. You come to work, you make the meals, you feed the hungry, you comfort the lonely, and you do it without expecting public praise.

The nation has not yet minted the coin with which to pay for such love; we've not struck the medal with which to reward your heroism. But those of us who walk the road to AIDS see you every day, nearby, caring for us. And we say to each other, and to all who will listen: "These are the heroes."

*Excerpt from "Remarks at Project Open Hand"*
*Address by Mary Fisher*
*San Francisco, California*
*Monday, August 1, 1994*

Groceries to be delivered by
Project Open Hand

*For a decade-and-a-half America at-large has said that AIDS is not our problem, not our disease. It belongs to "your" community or "their" community or no community at all, but it does not belong to "us." Fever by night and cancer by day—if it is AIDS, it is not ours. We have clung to our denial, passing judgment on those the virus finds, imagining that it belongs to those less worthy, less moral, less righteous, than ourselves. We have cherished our prejudices, loved our stigma, and forgotten that God makes some pilgrims strong so they can carry the weak.*

*Today, the San Francisco Giants demonstrate that AIDS is as all-American as Abner Doubleday's sport. No longer can we deny that this epidemic is all of ours. No longer must men and women and children hide in fear and shame as they grow weak and die. Because good men in San Francisco are not only baseball's Giants, but moral giants as well.*

*Excerpt from "Until There's a Cure Day"*
*Remarks at the San Francisco Giants Game*
*by Mary Fisher*
*San Francisco, California*
*Sunday, July 31, 1994*

# LOS ANGELES

## August 1994

The natural setting for caregiving is the family at home. It becomes dramatic when strangers are joined at death's gate. But caregiving is ordinary nurturing for most of us, most of our lives, most of the time. It's a mother drawing her infant to her breast, a father picking up his daughter when she's fallen, an aunt patiently spacing the fingers of her eight-year-old niece's hand on the piano keyboard. It's grandparents explaining our father's middle name. It's the conviction that we can go home, no matter what has happened.

But when families break down, for whatever reasons, or when we have no family, caregiving can be more precious than gold, and just as hard to find.

Los Angeles was sizzling in August, 1994 when I went to photograph caregivers. Heat and smog had settled in ahead of the Santa Ana winds that would only raise the temperatures in September. It was a mean heat, the kind that turns apartments into ovens and neighborhoods into war zones. There were rumors of riots.

Against that backdrop, I was shooting film of caregivers in programs

Jewel and Rue Thais-Williams

104

that were essentially devoted to one thing: creating family for those who needed family most.

**<u>Rue's House</u>**. I had heard the story before, but I wanted photographic evidence that this place really was Rue's house which she (Rue Thais-Williams) and her life partner, Jewel Thais-Williams, had converted into a home for women and children with AIDS. What I found was a woman as conventional as possible about family values in as unconventional a family as can be imagined.

Rue and Jewel are an African-American couple. They met, fell in love, and somewhere along the line noticed that African-American and Latino children represented two of the fastest-growing segments of the AIDS community in Los Angeles County.

I read their material before arriving with my cameras. The core of their philosophy was this: "The physical and mental health and welfare of mothers and their children, AIDS-infected or not, is better served by keeping the family together." To keep mothers and children

together in a unit, Rue and Jewel became the extended family whose house was "borrowed" for a while by those who needed it.

But this was not *Little House on the Prairie*. This was a program built on hardnosed in-fighting by two women who distrusted "the system" and intended to "save women" in the grip of everything from spousal abuse to drug addiction to the Los Angeles County judicial system.

Rue told me that she "never set out to be a care-giver." She just began collecting people who needed help. "Eventually we needed some place to put them."

Some women heard about Rue's House through informal networks, the grapevine. Some were dropped off by police or social workers or ex-residents. And some were toted into the house by Rue herself. When she would hear about a woman in prison with six kids and AIDS, she'd go argue for her release, round up the half-dozen children, and fill half the house in one night. She had stormed more than one social worker's office, demanding to know "by what right" they intended to take away children from mothers with AIDS. And when a young prostitute, infected, was being threatened by her pimp, Rue Thais-Williams found the young woman and her daughter, and—on the way home to Rue's House

☙ CORRESPONDENCE ☙

*September 28, 1996*

*Dear Mary,*

*To make a long story short, I walked out of my life in New Mexico and came home to take care of Gerald. In his passing, he taught me more about life and living than I would have ever learned on my own. We bonded in a way that comes only from the extreme experiences of foxholes, combat, and cataclysmic tragedy. He had no other family close to him. He had a limited support system. AIDS took over our lives completely, as you know it does, and I went through the whole range of emotions that goes along with this horrible disease. . . .*

*Just before Gerald passed away, we were having a talk and I asked him if there was anything I could do for him. I told him I would do anything I could. He thought for a minute and said, "Find a way to make a difference . . . ." Two days later he died in my arms.*

*A.L.*
*South Carolina*

Rue Thais-Williams

where they would stay—stopped by the pimp's corner to "explain why he never would do that again."

The mother of the children I photographed most at Rue's did not want her name published. But she was happy to tell me her story: She gave birth to a child in prison and, one week later, her baby girl was taken from her and put into foster care. "I knew I had AIDS," she said, "but I didn't know they could do this." They couldn't. Rue intervened.

Rue and those who served with her demonstrated every day Rue's House was open—it was closed in December of 1996 due to lack of funding—that caregiving isn't always sweetness. Sometimes it is tough, tough love.

**Chris Brownlie Hospice**. If no two caregivers are quite alike—and they aren't—neither are any two hospices.

Part of what made my visit to the Chris Brownlie Hospice remarkable were the people I met there: Sandra Shephard, Bruce Emery's caregiver, who spoke love with quiet, amazing eye contact. David Marrott, the masseuse, who cared for Danny Masa with heart and hands. And Janis Takamoto, a social worker, whose affection for

*I needed to stay home with Max and Zack tonight, but I wish I could be there, celebrating your retirement from APLA and your 40th birthday. I wanted to be there to laugh at the roasts and cry at the toasts, and to be part of the emotional crowd giving you a standing ovation when, finally, you are introduced. But most of all I wanted to be there for the same reason I always want to be near you. Because you not only do good things; you are, beyond all the good that you do, a very, very good man. And I love you.*

*Since I'm home tonight, I'm going to tell the boys what it could be like when they're grown up, when they've each become a man.*

*I'm going to say, "You could be like Uncle Phill." Because if they will keep their eyes fixed on you, they'll grow up seeing that when God makes a man truly strong, the man is gentle; when God makes a man courageous, the man has faith; and when God makes a man selfless, that man goes through life leaving a trail of love everywhere. . . .*

*I will pray tonight, and always, that when Max and Zack are grown, they will have your gentle strength, your faithful courage, and your selfless love. . . .*

*Letter from Mary Fisher*
*on the Retirement of Phill Wilson*
*April 25, 1996*

David Marrott

Clayton Lee Lyles and others was not a consequence of professional requirements. Each of them deserves a chapter of praise, and each of them would reject every sentence of it.

But behind the Chris Brownlie Hospice stands another caregiver, Chris Brownlie's caregiver, Phill Wilson.

Phill Wilson is the son, grandson, and great-grandson of African-American Baptist preachers. Founder of AIDS Project Los Angeles (known in the city as APLA) from which he only retired when his illness pulled him away from day-to-day duties, Phill is on a first-name basis with the powerhouses of the media and entertainment industries. He can tell you who makes commitments out of sincerity, who out of guilt, and who out of compassion. He can name the people "who will be there, no matter what, even if there are no cameras." He knows caregivers.

And he knows caregiving, because Chris Brownlie was Phill Wilson's partner. Phill loved Chris from this life into the next. And when a memorial for Chris was needed, what better or more loving tribute was possible than a hospice?

When the Family AIDS Network created its national caregivers award program, the first person we named to the caregiver selection committee was the easiest of all choices: Phill Wilson.

**<u>Tuesday's Child</u>**. She and her dark-eyed son both had AIDS. "How old are you?" I asked her while pulling off a lens cap. "Twenty. And he just turned two in June."

While I moved equipment around, looking for a place with enough light to take photographs, she told me her story of life with AIDS. She explained in Hispanic-accented English about being sick without reason, about doctors who misdiagnosed the causes. By the time she was tested, she was pregnant. "So they tell me to do an abortion, and I say no. I didn't want to kill the baby. I have him, and I thought he would come out negative. But he came positive. Now he has AIDS. Before, I thought it would be easier. But now he's here, and he has AIDS, and it's more hard."

More hard. So hard that she had wondered about suicide if the worst should happens. "When he was real sick and I feel so bad I said, 'You have to help me with the baby,' I tell God, because if you help me with the baby I won't kill myself. And then I say, 'Oh, sorry, I don't want

What AIDS looks like at twenty and two (mother and child with AIDS)

to say this.' God will get mad. So I take it back."

We talked about husbands with AIDS and teenagers who take risks. We talked about friends and then about family, about our sisters and brothers, about our children. We talked about being caregivers for our children. . . .

After time with her I spent time with Shevawn Avilla. Shevawn's son, Troy, had been born premature; he needed blood transfusions. He got AIDS.

Troy was six before the diagnosis was made. Shevawn traced the history of health crises that followed, a litany of hospitalizations and drugs and surgeries. She talked about Troy's relationship with his little brother, Aaron, about how Aaron worried that Troy would die, and how Troy grew angry because Aaron was growing up.

I was nearly done taking pictures of Shevawn with her children—Zoe, Aaron, and Maya—when Shevawn said, "I told him to fight." I asked what she meant.

"I told him to fight, you know, but when he got really, really tired, he just couldn't fight any more. He said he didn't want to die. But then he said, 'Well, it's not that bad. It's okay. It's okay. . . .'"

People had wanted to come and pray with Shevawn but she declined. She felt that God was angry with her, punishing her for something she must have done.

"But then this Scripture came into my head," she said, eyes brimming with tears. " 'In my Father's house are many mansions; if it were not so, I would have told you.' We've always lived in an apartment, you know, and the big American dream is to have a house. And here Troy is going to be the first one to move into a mansion. And I was all right with that."

Shevawn Avila with her children Zoe, Aaron, and Maya

# WASHINGTON, D.C.
## May & June 1997

Nearly three years had passed since I had taken a round of caregiver photographs. Everything had changed.

My art took a turn toward AIDS. For years I created and sold handmade paper paintings, mostly of flowers—large, colorful, buoyant flowers. But by late 1994 three things were blending in my art: handmade paper, photography, and AIDS. Instead of brilliant, soothing flowers, I found myself constructing life-size, furniture-like sculptures made mostly of wood and finished with photographs and handmade papers. A *New York Times* columnist wrote about my new art and the United States Senate invited me to have a one-woman exhibit of my sculptures to be displayed in the Senate Russell Building Rotunda. I created an exhibit called "Messages."

Looking back, two things seem worth observing: First, because I was using my photographs as components of other, larger pieces of art, I didn't think of the photographs themselves as the end-product. I saw them as a part of my medium, but not as things that could, or should, stand on their own. Second, when the Senate asked that I remove pieces from the "Messages" exhibit which some senators found offensive (notably, an ornate, coffin-like piece whose scroll bore the message "Let us unite in life, rather than death"), I was stunned. Senators vote on Articles of War, capital punishment, and abortion, but thought that, after hundreds of thousands of American AIDS deaths, a symbol of death was "inappropriate" in the halls of our national assembly.

The flap over "Messages" was not, in the broader scope of the epidemic, very important, but it was symbolic. Two decades into this epidemic, our leading statesmen don't want to think about its killing power. Individual senators and representatives have struggled to increase research for a cure and resources for the infected, but in recent years they have lost more than they have gained. The research being funded (and widely ballyhooed by the President) is not aimed at a cure; it's aimed at a preventative, which will leave those already infected without hope. Announcements about treatment breakthroughs have fueled misunderstandings and a mean division in the AIDS community between the "haves" and the "have nots." Those who "have" get drugs that may prolong their lives; those who "have not," don't.

Meanwhile, the virus has sailed into American communities of youth, color, and women, leaving in its wake decimated populations of hemophiliacs and gay men. The "average" American with AIDS today is younger and poorer than at any time in the past. Globally, the epidemic is forecast to erase 50,000,000 or more lives in the coming two decades; nationally, the AIDS community grows constantly larger as a result of ignorance, prejudice, fear, silence, and policies that successfully cloak the

*April 1996*

*Dear Mary,*

*I've loved all the guys I've cared for in the last years. But this time I think I got too close. And so, when I told you Friday evening that my caregiving had just ended, it wasn't because of burnout or weariness. It was just grief. The pain seemed so much more intense this time. Maybe it's a cumulative process. Each time I lose one, I lose them all again.*

*N.B.*
*[no return address]*

reality of death in the rhetoric of hope.

Many AIDS-related grassroots and community-based treatment centers now are mainstreamed into larger healthcare systems. When the gay community no longer saw AIDS as exclusively "its" problem, no other community stepped forward to say "it's ours!" Programs that once had the militant, feisty character of an embattled minority, staffed by volunteers who'd been qualified by their own sufferings (often with AIDS itself), now have been largely sanitized by government regulations and professionalized by those qualified by degrees.

For all these changes, one thing has not changed: the caregiver. He still rises in the night to care for someone he loves. She still drives through a snowstorm to calm someone she adores. They push the giggling child higher in the swing, read the newest bestseller to someone whose eyes have grown dim, turn a sweat-drenched body in the night— practitioners of the unseen acts of love.

It is always compassion that motivates true caregiving, never ambition or self-promotion. Such caregiving is as prevalent today as it was on a bone-chilling day some years ago when I asked a caregiver in Michigan if I could take her picture. We've all moved on. And wherever we've gone, there have been caregivers.

The media are delighted to report "news" (translated: hopeful research announcements) about AIDS. But there's nothing new about AIDS itself, including the caregiving. Which is probably why the stories of caregivers aren't plastered all over every day's edition of your local

Bevelyn Murray
with Joshua and William

116

newspaper. And why I decided to pick up my camera again, and shoot a few more pictures of exemplary caregivers.

These people are not newsworthy. They are merely heroic.

**Grandmother's Love**. Bevelyn Murray was not depressed. I met her in subsidized housing where she was living on a budget that made me blush. She cared for her son; he died of AIDS in 1992. She had cared for her daughter who was in prison when I visited. While waiting for her daughter to return, she took over care for her grandson Joshua, who was six and HIV-positive, and William, who was nine months and also HIV-positive. She was "happy" to have me "drop by to take pictures of my babies." When she picked up William, she held him with pride. When she cuddled the little boy, she closed her eyes, smiled and hummed. And when I was packing cameras to leave, she came to give me a hug I still can feel.

Grandmother Bevelyn Murray was full of faith, hope, and charity. She did not have self-pity, anger, or doubt about God. She told me she recently had begun volunteering as a caregiver for the AIDS ministry at her church "because God's given me so much, I want to give something back."

**Award-Winning Care**. Some years ago the Family AIDS Network, with which I work, began a national program to highlight, for the media and for financial support, the work of exemplary caregivers. Two of the early "winners" were Saptarishi Rice Boothe ("Rishi") and Janice R.

Boothe, partners in life and in caregiving.

It was easy to be with Janice and Rishi and their "buddies," Jim and Clayton, again. We first met when I'd presented Rishi and Jan with their national caregiver award, and I remembered laughing at their jokes about winning awards for something like loving people.

As I took pictures, we talked about holidays spent together and

times when relationships had grown too intense, and frayed. We talked about films and books and food. We talked about the joys of life and our curiosity about death and the people we've loved and lost.

Our conversation was perfectly ordinary, like what you'd hear over almost any family dinner table. Which is, almost precisely, the magic of powerful caregiving.

**The Family Kitchen**. Tim Kiernan was team captain for packing, the person at the Food & Friends kitchen who, three days a week, helped prepare meals for some 420 people with AIDS in Washington, D.C. It's serious work. He was paid nothing.

When I asked what motivated him, it proved to be a fairly long story. But the plot required only two sentences: "David was an artist. He was my partner for eighteen years and he died in November of 1995."

Some people have a hard time believing that good things can come out of bad. They should meet the family around this kitchen. They should watch Tim Kiernan and Karen Fitzgerald pack food for people who are hungry for calories and comfort.

I found Tim in the kitchen at Washington's Food & Friends program, getting lunches ready to "hit the street." Before I unpacked my cameras, I listened to Tim and his crew tell stories, joke, holler for more supplies, tease, and worry together ("Did anyone find out why Fred didn't answer the door yesterday?"). Someone started telling stories about food deliveries he'd made. He recalled the goofy, massive, African-

American man who answered the door in full make-up ("a Nell Carter look-alike") and persuaded two smaller, white volunteers to stand on his porch and sing "Happy Birthday" to him. Everyone laughed at the memory. Tim remembered deliveries to the grim apartment behind a basement furnace room in a filthy apartment complex ("I always felt there were rodents looking at me").

"We've become a family here," Tim said. Karen Fitzgerald, a member of the prep crew, explained that "some of us are gay and some of us have AIDS and some of us aren't and don't." But it's family.

I came expecting "another food kitchen." I wasn't prepared, I think, for the depth of commitment and the incredible histories these people began to unpack in front of me. I was touched. And I told them so. While they silently prepped and packed food, I spent two, maybe three minutes explaining how ter-rific they were, how important they were, how amazed I was. "I'm just bowled over by it," I admitted, as their hands fed packets with sandwiches and salad. "I think you are, each of you, heroes." I stopped for a moment, near tears. No one said anything for a moment. Then, without

Food & Friends

looking up, Karen spoke for the group.

"Thanks. . .that's really overblown."

**A Circle of Caregivers**. John Abbot, caregiver coordinator for Food & Friends, was Melvin Pippen's first AIDS caregiver. "Melvin is a character," he said as we sat waiting for Melvin to come back from a trip to the hospital. "I love Melvin. He was one of D.C.'s premier Diana Ross impersonators until he became ill."

I'd gone with John and Jennifer ("Jen") Anderson, who's Melvin's caregiver now, to meet Melvin at his apartment in the basement of his grandmother's home. As John and Jen and I waited outside, Melvin's grandmother, Mary Mider, sat in the house watching a succession of daily soap operas. I saw her peer out twice, but she showed no inclination to join us.

Jen talked about "people who have shaped me," referring not to grade-school teachers or champions she wanted to imitate, but to those for whom she's cared since joining Food & Friends four years ago. John talked about the one week out of every eight that he takes Interluken II and gets sick. "I have to take sedatives and pain killers; I'm out of it, way down—need my own caregiver for twenty-four hours." Jen explained why John is so extraordinary; John asked Jen if she were still buying prescriptions for her clients with her own money.

Finally Mary Mider came out and joined us. She was gracious and had a quiet elegance about her. She told me that Melvin used to sing in

Jennifer Anderson, Melvin
Pippen and Mary Mider

the choir at her church. "He used to make everybody happy by his songs. He has a gift." She shook her head. "But he won't go with me anymore. It makes me sad."

Melvin finally came home. AIDS was having its way with him. It had reduced his physical stamina but had not diminished his character. He was energetic and animated. We went downstairs with Jennifer to take pictures. While the film caught images of Jen and Melvin, I caught an earful of complaints Melvin had against his grandmother.

I had finished shooting film when Melvin came up to me. Jen had gone upstairs to see John, so we were alone. "You know, she's the one who raised me," he said, pointing upstairs. "She's the one who gave me my morals. She's the one who always loved me, and I've always loved her, and it's just sometimes I take it out on her." He was crying softly. "Really, I just love her."

We walked upstairs together and Mary Mider was there, waiting. Melvin walked up and gave her a kiss. She smiled, patted him, and walked away. I followed her to ask if she'd sign a release, so I could use a photo I'd taken earlier. She took the pen and, without looking up, said softly, "I love him, you know. He doesn't think I do. I care for him, but he just doesn't think I do."

"He knows," I said to her. "He knows." I reached out to give her a hug and she leaned in to return it. "Let me give you a blessing," she said, whispering a prayer I couldn't quite hear. But I could feel it in my soul.

**Stewart McKinney House**. Stewart B. McKinney was a Connecticut congressman who died of AIDS. In the months of his illness, he was cared for by his wife, the indestructible Lucie McKinney.

Stewart McKinney has been dead for nearly a decade. But Lucie

*We should be ashamed of ourselves. Like evangelists caught in cheap motels with bad magazines, we are where we ought not to be. Nearly two decades into an epidemic that has killed hundreds of thousands of Americans, we have gathered to discuss how many more should die. I regret that we have come to this point and, as an American, I am ashamed of it. And I want you to be ashamed too. We should never have gotten ourselves to the place we find ourselves, and we should get out of this as soon as possible.*

*Excerpt from "If Not Now. . ."*
*Address by Mary Fisher*
*Congressional AIDS Drug Assistance*
*Program Forum*
*Washington, D.C.*
*Thursday, April 17, 1997*

McKinney, small of stature with a mountain of determination, has kept his spirit alive. She's achieved this by writing letters cajoling and shaming legislators into supporting needed AIDS programs. She's fought local zoning that would have prevented AIDS organizations from providing services. And she continues to keep his spirit alive by breathing life and constant support into the Stewart McKinney House in the shadow of Stewart's one-time congressional office. Here, six (usually Hispanic) HIV-positive mothers and their children find respite and compassion.

And here Stephanie McAllister has become a caregiver. Was it a private trauma that turned her toward caregiving? Not even close:

> I graduated from college, went and lived in Spain for a year and came back. I was looking for a position in which I could use psychology and Spanish and I saw an ad for a bilingual person to care for people with AIDS. So I'm the freak person who actually got a job through the classifieds, that "one in a million" chance.
>
> I had only intended to stay a year. Here I am, three years already. It's been so wonderful I can't imagine leaving. Every year I put it off. I can't imagine leaving. Not now.

I was tired when we arrived at the Stewart McKinney House. It's easy, when you're tired, to have conversations like the one I had here, with Christine, about letting AIDS wear us down until we just want to end it all.

But that was the slump. The message of this place isn't weariness. It's

pluck and stamina, the characteristics that have enabled congressional wife and mother Lucie McKinney to become a red-haired dynamo with whom policymakers must reckon.

Lucie McKinney is not a caregiver in the conventional sense. But she is a caregiver with a mission which, in many ways, is common among caregivers. She remembers. And she'll not let others forget. She will not let her husband's death be meaningless.

**Blind Faith**. I didn't know quite what to expect when I arrived at the HIV Community Coalition offices to meet with members of Blind Faith, a support group made up almost entirely of people who've served time and are HIV-positive. What I found was what I've found in support groups around the globe over the past decade or more: people committed to living a better life by enabling others to do the same.

The mother of all support groups is, of course, Alcoholics Anonymous. In its wake have come dozens of other "anonymous" groups and twelve-step programs. We begin our participation in these groups by admitting we cannot control our own lives. We need to live by something other than self-control, because self-control hasn't worked.

Cochise Robertson-El, the founder and leader of Blind Faith, introduced me to the group. For more than an hour, we exchanged our life stories, one by one, going around the circle. At the end, Cochise closed the meeting by talking about what happens when we care for each other:

Kenneth E. Blackson-El, Fredrick Johnson, Yvonne Green, Cynthia James, Cochise Robertson-El, Willie James Byrd, Wanda James, and Leon Williford at Blind Faith

127

We came from prison, from drugs, from alcohol, from the streets. And we've become employable people. Willie Byrd, he's working. Kenny, a man who started his own business. Yvonne, who once didn't have anything—couldn't have gotten out of D.C.—just came back from Albuquerque. Fred, a guy who came from San Quentin, who found his way home by blind faith. There's a sister showing compassion and mercy for her sister, so she got involved. . . . We will not quit until we have stopped the spread of this virus in our community, and in the prison setting. We are the underprivileged, the voice that's never been heard at the table where policies are being made. . . .

So long as we wake up—whether we've got sores and lesions on us, or we're losing weight, or whatever's happening—we hear the call, and the duty is to live. When we respond to that call and take on that duty, there's a power higher than us that's going to give us the energy and strength to succeed.

Caregiving isn't about helping us to die. It's about enabling us to live one day at a time.

*For twenty years this nation has treated persons with AIDS as uniquely responsible for their own condition. Despite what we know about smoking and cancer, we have not done to smokers what we have done to persons with AIDS. Despite what we know about diet, we have not done to heart-attack sufferers what we have done to persons with AIDS. Despite what we know about bucking horses and skydiving, we have not done to Christopher Reeves what we have done to persons with AIDS.*

*So deep has the stigma been, so controversial the epidemic, that more than a hundred thousand Americans had died of the disease before an American President dared say the word "AIDS" in public. Tens of thousands of obituaries have lied about the cause of death, out of families' fear or shame. And shame is, indeed, the issue. How do I explain to my sons Max and Zack their father's death and my disease, on one hand, and the nation's response on the other, with anything less than shame?*

*Excerpt from "If Not Now. . ."*
*Address by Mary Fisher*
*Congressional AIDS Drug Assistance Program Forum*
*Washington, D.C.*
*Thursday, April 17, 1997*

# BIRMINGHAM

June 1997

I'd been put on protease inhibitors a few months earlier and, as the side effects kicked in, I felt increasingly wretched.

On Thursday, June 5, I was scheduled to be the commencement speaker at Wayne State University Medical School in Detroit. I could not make the trip. So—at the Dean's invitation—I wrote a letter to be read by my friend Debbie Dingell, apologizing for my absence and explaining it ("The reason, in a word, is AIDS").

> It is not the AIDS virus, exactly, which has kept me away from you; it is the therapy we're employing to fight it. I'm wrestling with prescriptions that may save my life and with side effects of those prescriptions which make me wonder if life is worth saving. I am where most people with AIDS arrive at some point in the course of their illness: weary beyond imagination, frustrated to the point of rage, and discouraged. Mary Fisher—the girl next door, the blonde Republican, the woman who produces encouraging photographs and delivers inspirational speeches—Mary Fisher is struggling to care about whether she lives or dies.

The national news media picked on that paragraph and played it up a bit. I wish they had paid more attention to the actual theme of the letter: the call for healers to be caregivers.

"What lies before you now is the prospect of being not merely a healer but of being a hero," I wrote to the graduating physicians. "I know physicians who are heroes, and I know some who are not. The difference between them is character."

I held out my expectations for them, to become wounded healers, men and women who would be willing to be vulnerable to pain:

> I am not inspired by those who can identify the sicknesses but cannot identify with the sick. I do not need another physician who is clinically precise and emotionally detached; whose concern for my well-being is exceeded by her concern for my insurance; whose primary purpose in life is to secure enough money to perfect his long putts and slippery chip shots. I want a physician who cares deeply about his patients, who is panic-stricken when her efforts fail. When you tell me that my child's cancer is back, I want your voice to break. When you tell my children they are orphans, I want you to hold them both until you all stop crying.

I admitted that "I learned the model of wounded healers and vulnerable physicians from Dr. Michael Saag, an eminent AIDS researcher and an extraordinary physician," although I did not mention that Michael is my cousin. I told the story of Michael and a patient, Billy, who died of AIDS. And I closed the letter:

If I had a single graduation gift to give each of you, it would be this: I would instill in you the gift of vulnerability. I would make you not less human in the face of suffering, but more. I'd ask that when you cannot cure the pain and suffering, you stand ready to share it. In short, I'd beg for you the courage to be weak and the strength to endure your own weaknesses, without running from those of us who've come to you for healing. It was not in Michael's hands to cure Billy, but it was in his soul to love him—and in such love there is a healing beyond science, and beyond words.

Michael Saag, M.D. with Ben Davis

**<u>1917 Clinic</u>**. I first visited the University of Alabama's Birmingham AIDS clinic in 1993. My mother had persuaded me to go because she was convinced that my cousin, whom I hardly knew as an adult, had become one of the world's great AIDS researchers. Two things surprised me during my visit: first, the clinic was named for its street address, not its date of founding; and, second, my mother was right.

The 1917 Clinic is the setting both for laboratory research and clinical care for persons with AIDS. Its hallways envelope AIDS patients who are candidates for the newest drug tests, and staff who are candidates for the highest awards in their fields. But all the talk is about the drugs, not the awards. In fact, even that isn't true. The focus here is not drugs. It's people.

## Working with What's Left.

Benjamin ("They call me Ben") Davis was in commercial real estate in Atlanta for seventeen years "before I got this neuropathy and everything just went down the tubes." He'd had AIDS for a long time, but his inability to walk was new. And it was frightening, because he needed to walk. His mother was his primary caregiver, and "she already has one son with Lou Gehrig's Disease. He needs constant care. So I need to be able to get around. I need to."

Michael Saag, M.D.
with Ben Davis

Ben Davis, although his mother's son, is not a child. He craves independence. He alternates between praising his mother ("She's a rock. . .a great caregiver. . .would do anything. . .just gives, gives, gives") and feeling guilt ("She's seventy-four! She's at a period in life where she should be enjoying life. All her friends are going around the world . . ."). As I listened to him talk, I realized the yin-yang of being cared for: we need it, we resent it, we admire it, we feel guilt for it.

Midway through my conversation with Ben, Mike joined us. He went into physician-speak, that almost sing-song lingo that doctors often use when they recount our medical history. Without referring to charts, Mike began listing the arsenal of drugs he and Ben had tried together, and the constant monitoring of T-cells and viral loads. He remembered coming back from the Berlin Conference on AIDS in 1993, "when everyone was saying all hope was lost," and discovering that a medical protocol he was trying with Ben had worked. His viral load—the measure of how much "AIDS virus" we have in our bodies—had dropped dramatically. "We'd never seen anything like this before." Mike was getting enthused. "This was historic." His voice was up. "This was phenomenal!"

But it hadn't lasted. Here, today, Ben was back again, now with neuropathy.

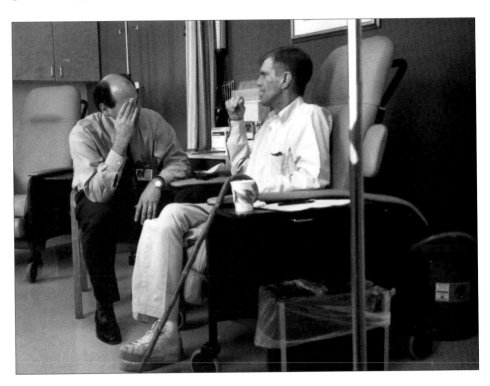

Michael Saag, M.D.
with Ben Davis

Mike was subdued as, together, they talked about what could be learned from what doesn't work, how Ben was contributing to science even by failing physically. "It's just us, all together, working together, to learn more," said Mike.

Michael Saag, M.D. with Ben Davis

Ben said he'd like to be able to walk again. Mike said he hoped "we can get there." There were a few minutes of awkward silence in which it was clear no promises were being made. Ben said he understood. It was trial-and-error. But he was up for it. If he couldn't take another step physically, maybe he could make another contribution—to science.

Ben's mother has been his caregiver. Mike has been Ben's caregiver. Others may also serve as his caregivers. But in what Ben is willing to do for science, he has been my caregiver.

"I'm ready, willing, and able," he said, picking up everyone's mood. "Whatever there is to do. Whatever's left."

**<u>The Rabbi</u>**. Rabbi Cyndie Culpeper is a woman with AIDS. Before she was a rabbi, she was a nurse. A needle slipped, once, which is how she became a woman with AIDS. We met first when she sent me a letter, near the time she was preparing to tell her congregation that she had AIDS. She'd gotten sick since that time, and had moved to Birmingham to be closer to the 1917 Clinic.

I wanted to take photographs, but it was hard to put the camera between us. So we talked, two women with AIDS, about drugs and side-effects, and side-effects, and more side-effects. We sympathized with each other, knowing exactly what indignities the other had endured and had never wanted to tell the outside world.

We talked about the boxes of prescriptions that line our lives and punctuate our days, and our common conviction that our lives are insanely dominated by pills.

Then Culpeper pulled herself up and said: "Well, you know, it could be worse. There's this old story. . . ." She sounded like a rabbi again:

> A guy in a small village came to his rabbi and said, "Things are terrible at home. Too crowded, too noisy, everything's miserable." So the rabbi says, "You got a goat?" "Yeah," says the guy. "Bring the goat into the house and come back next week." So the guy moves the goat into the house and goes back in a week. "You got a cow?" asks the rabbi. "Yeah, I got a cow." "Move the cow into the house and come back next week." So the guy moves the cow into the house and goes back in a week. That week it's chickens. The next week it's something else. Now things are really bad at home. So the rabbi finally says, "Okay, take out the goat, take out the cow, take 'em all out and

Michael Saag, M.D.
with Rabbi Cyndie Culpeper

come back next week." So the guy comes back to the rabbi the next week and says things have never been more wonderful. "Everything's great!" he says.

Sometimes, between the pills and the tests and the confusion, life gets a little noisy and crowded. But, declares Rabbi Cyndie Culpeper, "it could be worse."

**Mom**. Mike had suggested that I take a photograph of Barbara Goggans-Martin, a caregiver whose son, Eddie, was being treated at the 1917 Clinic.

Eddie was in a wheelchair. He had been told, moments earlier, that he had CMV (*Cytomegalovirus*) in both eyes. The sight in his left eye had disappeared completely a week earlier; there was hope, maybe, for his right. His caregiver, his mother, was with him.

Momma and I have been with AIDS for a long time, because my brother Charles had AIDS and passed away February 19, 1991. He lived in New York for about twelve years. He was with ACT UP in New York. He came back to Birmingham and he was the only ACT UP person in Birmingham and he did some amazing things. There were some federal judges—this was like 1987 or something—and they said they wouldn't allow anyone who was HIV-positive to be in their courtrooms. So Charles went down, and he sat down in court, and he was a one-man protest, and he got it changed. . . .

We talked for a while, Eddie and Eddie's mother and I. For all the dying that they've seen, all the sickness they've endured together, all the hours she's bent over sons who were fighting for life, I never heard a complaint from her. When she described something difficult, she spoke of challenges that had been overcome. She had no sense of her own courage or dignity.

Eddie's mother's eyes never left her son. She was concerned, but it wasn't a look of concern that I saw. It was joy in the memory of Charles' courage, and in Charles' brother's memory of it, too.

"I'm so proud of Charles," she said, turning to me, speaking almost as if Charles were still alive. "And I'm proud of him, too"—looking at Eddie—"because he's done some fine things as well."

If I asked her about being a caregiver, she wouldn't have known what I meant. She only knew about being a mother, and exulting in her sons' achievements.

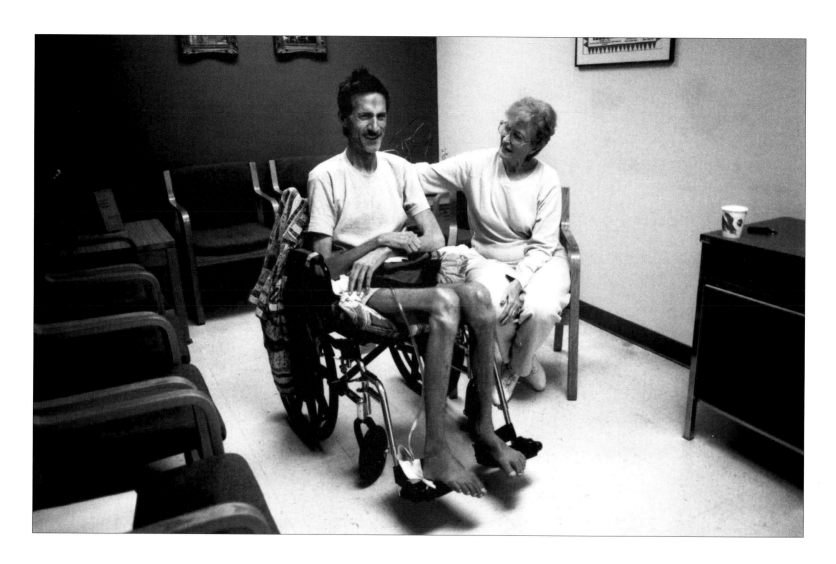

Eddie Goggans with
his mother, Barbara

**<u>The Essence of Being a Physician</u>**. If you didn't know that
Michael Saag was a Jewish doctor in Birmingham, Alabama, judging by
the look and sound of him, you'd say he was a Chamber of Commerce
executive from Louisville or a high school band leader from Kansas City.

Balding, always "watching the weight," with a face that's a movie screen on which every emotion is projected, he loves to tell stories, to play with the children, to laugh. Just being near him is healing.

We were sitting, talking, with one of his patients. I was preparing to take the last photograph for this book. And Michael was answering my question, "How do you feel about your patients?"

"Every patient is special," he said, sparkling, smiling. "Research patients are extra special. They go the extra mile. There may be some gain in it, they may get access to a new drug, but you never know if that new drug is going to work or if it is going to kill your liver. It's pioneer stuff, a frontier thing."

He looked past me to the patient with whom we'd been talking, and he grew a little more serious. "They do more things, the research patients. They get more blood drawn. . . .

"As I follow people, over time, we develop a friendship." Mike had now started down a personal road, looking not at me but at the other person in the room, the other person with AIDS here, the other one who trusted him the way I trust him. "I learn about his family, I learn about what he does. I learn about the trials and tribulations he faces every day." Mike was spacing his sentences now, trying not to let his emotions show. "And that's nice. And that's important. And that's the essence of what being a physician is about. But. . .but. . .sometimes. . . ."

Sometimes caregivers weep.

*April 27, 1994*

*Dear Mary,*

*You are brave, understanding, nice and a super hugger. I think about you all the time and pray that you're healthy.*

*If only there were more people like you, I wouldn't have to live a double life. Because the hardest thing in the world to do is to have to have a disease and have to keep it a secret. I always feel like screaming out, "I have AIDS and I'm a twelve-year-old kid and you could have it too!" That probably sounds stupid too, but that's how I feel. It's hard to keep the secret.*

*D.*
*Florida*

*We do not blame you for our virus; we blame no one, even those who infected us. Millions of women with AIDS contracted the virus the way we'd hoped to conceive children, in loving relationships. But it's hard not to grow angry at the slow pace of research, especially for women. How is it possible this late in the epidemic to have so few women in trials that we don't yet know what works and what doesn't? How is it possible, so late, that we cannot distinguish which symptoms are PMS and which are HIV—which belong to the virus, which to our hormones, and which to your drugs?*

*Excerpt from "Letter to a Young Physician"*
*Open Letter by Mary Fisher*
*Read at Wayne State University Medical School Commencement*
*Detroit, Michigan*
*Thursday, June 5, 1997*

. . . *The rate of dying has slowed for all population groups in the U.S. except one: women. Why do you suppose women, especially women of color and women of poverty, are dying faster than others? When I've asked them, they've explained that, given a choice between feeding their children and buying their drugs, they prefer to feed their children. Some have measured the cost of taking medications which will make them sick, and realized they cannot care for children while enduring the side-effects; they stopped taking medications. And many won't consider life-extending drugs because, to get them, they'd need to tell the truth about their illness. They'd need to admit they have AIDS. And in American culture, a woman with AIDS is a "leper." She's seen as a woman without virtue, without modesty, without value—a dirty woman with a dirty disease. Women are dying fastest, I think, because, given time to think it over, more women than men have decided that life itself is not worth the price of the battle.*

*Excerpt from "Letter to a Young Physician"*
*Open Letter by Mary Fisher*
*Read at the Wayne State University*
*Medical School Commencement*
*Detroit, Michigan*
*Thursday, June 5, 1997*

# PROGRAM PROFILES

*There are literally thousands of programs around the country providing care for those who have HIV and AIDS. The dedicated people who work in these programs and those who are friends and family are sometimes paid, sometimes volunteer, but all work from a place in the heart. I was able to visit just a few of these individuals and programs. I include a brief description of the programs here as a small sample and example of the vast network of phenomenal caregiving.*

# Grand Rapids

### *Hospice of Greater Grand Rapids*

Since 1980, Hospice of Greater Grand Rapids has served more than 1,500 people in life's final stages by offering comforting care and support for both patients and families.

"Care is based on the belief that every patient and family has values and beliefs which must be respected," the agency's brochure declares.

"The patient is in control of the decision-making process, including the plan of care."

The Hospice helps people with all kinds of terminal illnesses control symptoms and pain without hastening or postponing death. It also offers one-to-one counseling, support groups, grief recovery seminars, and a personal correspondence program to patients' family members.

Hospice of Greater Grand Rapids will care for patients at home or in one of its two residential programs: the Hospice Care Center or Home of Hope.

### *Home of Hope*

Home of Hope takes an unabashedly Christian approach to dying and death. The cover of the agency's brochure quotes the Apostle Paul's first letter to the Thessalonians: "I want you to know what happens to a Christian when he dies so that when it happens, you will not be full of sorrow as are those who have no hope."

Home of Hope tries to surround its eighteen residents with things they enjoy: twenty-four-hour visitation, even for pets; personal room decorations; a bird feeder outside every window and a duck pond and nature trail out back; a pianist playing favorite hymns each week.

Hospice care continues for families for more than a year after the death of a loved one, with support groups, grief recovery seminars and referral to pastoral care.

# Boston

### *Rosie's Place*

The tag line for the Rosie's Place logo is "Creating Solutions"—a mission fulfilled through providing unconditional love and support blended with practical resources and opportunities. As a result, the homeless women served by Rosie's Place find security, independence, and dignity for themselves and their families.

Established in 1974, Rosie's Place was the first drop-in center and emergency shelter for women in the United States. In recent years, the demand for services at Rosie's Place has continued to increase, in part due to the increasing number of women who are HIV-positive and require a number of services beyond health needs. It is conservatively estimated that over thirty percent of the women served by Rosie's Place are HIV-positive.

Given the complex nature of the women's needs, the staff at Rosie's Place meets each woman one-on-one to seek individualized solutions through legal advocates, housing and job-search specialists, nurses, and rape crisis counselors. In addition, the staff and 400 volunteers provide services, such as nutritional meals, for up to 150 women and children every day. An on-site food pantry distributes additional staples.

Rosie's Place includes not only a drop-in shelter but also extended-stay housing and permanent residence opportunities. Because of the growing number of homeless women with HIV, a residence for up to ten women living with HIV/AIDS was opened in 1994. The women are given support and assistance in making life decisions regarding medical care, child care, and financial matters. Other services, such as the coordination of medical care, counseling, nutritional services, education programs, and transportation, also are provided.

### The Children's AIDS Program

The Children's AIDS Program (CAP) offers a licensed day-care setting for twenty-nine young children who either have HIV/AIDS or have family members with the disease.

Based in a hospital, CAP affords clients easy access to medical care and psychological counseling. But by providing a nursery or kindergarten atmosphere, CAP can make special feeding and physical therapy seem part of a preschooler's routine.

The free program, established in 1987, gives infected adults a chance to keep the family together as much as possible as it unites against the vagaries of AIDS. CAP also lets parents continue working or schooling even if their child's needs exceed those of a traditional day-care program. And if parents die, CAP is there to help foster parents or relatives care for the children who are left behind.

### Mission Hill Hospice

Mission Hill Hospice (MHH) opened with a flood of publicity in 1989 as one of the country's first hospices specializing in care for terminal AIDS patients.

Less than a decade later, though, Mission Hill had become a victim of its rapid rise in popularity, former clinical director Pat Gibbons said. It was in debt because it didn't stage a capital campaign to offset its large mortgage before it opened. It didn't have guidelines for defining its admission criterion of "terminal within six months." And the hospice was not equipped to provide residential care for people with AIDS who were ill, but not terminal—a condition increasingly the norm as protease inhibitors turn AIDS into a chronic illness.

Started as a collaboration between Hospice West of suburban Boston and the local AIDS Action Committee, Mission Hill's staff of forty provided care for up to eighteen people in its two-story home. A few years later, the hospice closed the second floor and reduced the number of beds to nine. In January of 1997, Mission Hill Hospice shuttered its doors.

While it was open, though, the hospice was recognized nationwide for its outstanding care. Mission Hill staff understood and respected each person's unique interests and needs. "At MHH, a person's history began when they came through our doors," Gibbons said. "Fortunately, other agencies in Boston still provide services like those offered at Mission Hill."

# Atlanta

### Haven House

Haven House doesn't look like a place where people go to die. It sometimes does happen there, but Kathryn Middleton, vice-president and co-director of nursing, stresses that Haven House is a place to live.

Any signs that medical treatment occurs here are carefully, lovingly disguised. One notices the colorful quilts from home—not the hospital beds underneath. Medical apparatus is hidden behind antique furniture. Each bedroom has hardwood floors, a fireplace, and old photographs on the walls.

The renovated home with the roomy front porch has housed hundreds of terminal AIDS patients, as well as some not needing the intensive care of a hospital, yet not strong enough to go home. The ten-bed facility offers around-the-clock skilled-nursing care.

Middleton founded Haven House with friend Metta Johnson, co-director of nursing, and two others in early 1992 to provide "interim care," gently delivered by people with an intimate understanding of what residents are going through, who help with pain management, emotional counseling, and peer support.

### Atlanta Interfaith AIDS Network's Common Ground Program

Founded in 1989, the Atlanta Interfaith AIDS Network, Inc. (AIAN) is a coalition of churches and synagogues that joined forces to address the AIDS crisis from a faith perspective.

The people behind AIAN employ at least three major tools in building that bridge: care teams and pastoral care, a day-activity home, and educational services.

AIAN's AIDS Care Teams provide compassionate, non-judgmental care and practical support to people with AIDS. Care Teams develop in congregations that have begun to educate themselves about HIV/AIDS and are ready to put their faith into action. The teams address spiritual, physical, and emotional needs of people with AIDS. While pastoral care also is offered by AIAN in the form of counseling, spiritual nurturing, and comfort, AIAN does not teach or prefer any particular religion or faith experience.

Finally, AIAN is committed to educating the faith community about HIV/AIDS. Part of that educational process involves encouraging people of faith to minister to those affected by HIV in non-judgmental and compassionate ways.

## Project Open Hand

When Atlanta artist Michael Edwards returned from the 1987 AIDS March on Washington, D.C., he knew he wanted to help those infected with and affected by HIV/AIDS. He just wasn't sure how.

He started delivering meals to fourteen homebound people with AIDS on behalf of a local agency that received leftover food from restaurants, caterers, soup kitchens, and homeless shelters. When one day the meals didn't seem nutritionally proper for people with AIDS, he threw them out and replaced them with meals from a restaurant.

"All the while," Edwards said, "I was wondering why we were not cooking the meals ourselves."

Not long after that, Edwards attended a display of the Names Project Memorial AIDS Quilt and learned about another meal delivery program: Project Open Hand. After flying to San Francisco to meet with the founder, Ruth Brinker, he started an Atlanta chapter in the same way Brinker had started hers: to serve a small group of people by preparing meals in a church basement.

On September 12, 1988, the agency prepared its first fourteen meals in the kitchen of St. Bartholomew's Episcopal Church. Today, about 100 volunteers help Project Open Hand in Atlanta cook and deliver two meals daily to more than 550 people with AIDS and their dependent children.

# Rikers Island

## *Rikers Island STEP Program*

Women inmates on Rikers Island are able to shorten their terms and qualify for community service by participating in the "Self-Taught Empowerment and Pride" (STEP) Program. It's a creative and intense effort to raise prisoners' sense of self-worth, to help them to adopt and pursue goals, and to focus them on a lifestyle that is clean and sober and productive.

When inmates complete the STEP Program, there is a commencement ceremony to which family and special guests can be invited. Since most inmates have not finished their formal educations, the STEP graduation ceremony is an important "first" in their lives. For some, it's the strongest evidence they can offer in defense of their self worth.

# West Palm Beach

### *The Children's Place and Connor's Nursery, Inc.*

The Children's Place and Connor's Nursery, Inc. are dedicated to providing a loving home for the care and treatment of abused, abandoned, neglected, and HIV-positive infants and children. Reaching out to the community with healing guidance and compassion for families also is a commitment of the organization, which summarizes its goal: "to protect and nurture children as well as support and strengthen families."

Connor's Nursery provides both short- and long-term care as well as respite care for up to twenty infants and children with HIV/AIDS. Established in 1990, Connor's Nursery "provides these special children with the very best quality of life possible and, above all, offers the necessary support to keep the family together."

The Children's Place, which has two locations, operates twenty-four hours a day as a crisis shelter, providing a safe haven for infants and children through age six who have been removed from potentially dangerous situations. The two centers can care for up to twenty-four children; unfortunately, many are turned away daily because the shelters are at capacity.

In addition to these two programs, the agency offers a facility for children whose mothers are in a residential substance-abuse treatment program, an on-site preschool focusing on children with special needs, an outreach program providing families in crisis with resources such as food and housing, and a support group for parents that offers skills building, guidance, and counseling.

# New York City

## *Iris House*

In recent years, deaths due to AIDS have been on the decline among men of every racial group. But the number of AIDS deaths increased by three percent in 1996 among women, who now make up about twenty percent of AIDS cases.

Iris House in East Harlem was founded in 1991 to offer social services specifically for HIV-infected women and their families.

Established by the Women and AIDS Working Group of the Office of the Manhattan Borough President, Iris House has three main goals: to offer health and nutrition services and other "quality-of-life" assistance, to educate policy makers and health-and-human-services providers about the unique problems facing women with AIDS, and to advocate for changes in policy and programs to better serve women and families infected and affected by AIDS.

With family case management, Iris House offers support groups, stress management classes, legal counseling, nutritional assessments, home and hospital visits, child-care, and referrals for substance-abuse treatment, housing, welfare, medical care, and other services.

In September of 1993, the agency started its first full year of operation in a newly-renovated site in East Harlem that includes child-care facilities, a kitchen, and a resource library.

### STANDUP Harlem

See page 66.

# Kansas City

### SAVE Home

SAVE Home is the original creation of SAVE, Inc., a group of Kansas City businesspeople who wanted to provide permanent, low-cost, non-institutional housing for people with AIDS.

The home is still the only AIDS-specific residence/hospice in Missouri. Since 1987, more than 375 people have lived in SAVE Home's eight private bedrooms with attention from twenty-four hour healthcare staff. Hundreds of others have benefitted from the home's nutritional counseling and supply of medical equipment.

SAVE, Inc. arranges dual occupancy leases for assisted and independent living, and runs Gilligan Home, which houses three large, formerly homeless HIV/AIDS families. The agency also offers financial aid to those at risk of homelessness and helps families find affordable housing near social services. SAVE's Prairie Home and Cropsey Place are newly constructed and have furnished apartment buildings with rents based on ability to pay.

# San Francisco

### *Project Open Hand*

What started out as a lone woman cooking meals in a church basement for seven people with AIDS has grown into the world's largest food provider for people with symptomatic HIV and AIDS.

Project Open Hand, begun in 1985 by Meals on Wheels manager Ruth Brinker, now provides daily prepared meals, groceries, and nutrition education to more than 3,200 people each month.

The agency knows, and its dietitians teach, that a healthy diet improves a person's chance for long-term survival, even against the AIDS virus and potent drug treatments. Project Open Hand will custom-design menus for particular medical problems or personal preferences, including soft, bland, renal, vegetarian, low fat, low fiber, low lactose, and diabetic. Chefs also make special holiday meals and birthday cakes.

More than 1,700 volunteers prepare, bag, and deliver meals and keep track of clients. In 1995-1996, Project Open Hand delivered 560,480 meals, distributed 70,940 bags of groceries at food banks, home-delivered 39,707 bags of groceries, and served 5,881 clients. Nearly ninety percent of clients have an income of less than $900 per month.

### *Shanti Hospice*
See page 99.

# Los Angeles

### *Tuesday's Child*
When the health of a parent with AIDS declines, the children suffer too. Often, the parent can't afford some basic necessities, can't offer emotional support, and sometimes loses custody. Siblings and parents of infected children often can't find help, either.

Tuesday's Child, which has offices in Culver City and Long Beach, California, has a Necessities Assistance Program(NAP) providing families with diapers, baby food, infant formula, cribs, clothes, furniture, and other basic living necessities—even donated appliances. The NAP program also helps pay for rent, utilities, and, far too often, burial expenses.

A Family Events Program offers recreation and family time to ease the emotional burden of AIDS and caregiving. Christmas presents, Thanksgiving food baskets, movies, field trips, and other group outings provide a network of peer support.

By helping to reduce the financial, emotional, and material burden, Tuesday's Child tries to allow parents to "turn their attention to the consuming medical involvement demanded by HIV infection or an AIDS diagnosis."

Tuesday's Child serves more than 1,000 children from about 500 families. Nearly half of the registered families have annual incomes of less than $5,000; nearly ninety percent live on less than $15,000 per year. More than sixty percent of the households have both a primary caregiver and a child infected with HIV.

### Rue's House
See page 106.

### Chris Brownlie Hospice
See page 108.

# Washington, D. C.

### Food & Friends
Up to eighty percent of deaths from AIDS are related to hunger and malnutrition. Food & Friends, located in the most densely AIDS-infected city in the nation, provides free, home-made meals to homebound people with AIDS.

Each week, Monday through Saturday, about 500 volunteers

deliver three meals daily to more than 500 clients. With its Groceries to Go program, Food & Friends delivers a week's worth of meals at a time to nearly 200 more clients. Since May of 1989, Food & Friends has served more than 1.5 million meals. Over the last five years, the annual meal total has increased more than twenty-fold.

Most of the agency's clients live below the poverty level, with incomes of less than $550 per month. A client's health, living situation and dietary needs are reviewed, and delivery service usually starts the next day.

Professional chefs, with help from kitchen volunteers, prepare nutritionally balanced breakfasts, lunches, and dinners in Food & Friends' 12,000-square-foot kitchen and classroom building. Five part-time drivers visit thirteen drop-off sites, where volunteers pick up the meals and distribute them on seventy-five delivery routes in a 750-square-mile area around Washington, including suburban Maryland and northern Virginia. The Groceries to Go program covers more than 5,000 square miles, reaching into rural Maryland and Virginia.

To pay for its meal delivery service, Food & Friends receives $3.4 million in grants, including government funds covered under the Ryan White CARE Act.

### Stewart McKinney House
See page 124.

### Blind Faith
See page 127.

# Birmingham

### *University of Alabama-Birmingham 1917 Clinic*

The AIDS epidemic constantly shifts its targets. By historical happenstance, the disease started its rampage in this country among white urban males. Now, though, AIDS in America is bearing down on women and people of color, and lately has expanded most in the southeastern United States.

The University of Alabama-Birmingham Medical Center serves as a major medical referral center in the state and, as the AIDS epidemic settled in the region, the Center saw the need to establish the 1917 Clinic.

Since 1988 the Clinic has offered patient care; social support and counseling; clinical and other scientific research; education, especially of health care providers; and community outreach.

The benefits of such a centralized clinic are clear: It provides a resource for physicians and other healthcare professionals; and it allows 110 clinical investigators to have a steady pool of patients and specimens to track. By enrolling as many patients as possible in clinical trials, scientists are able to rigorously assess treatment success and side- effects.

Since its founding, the Clinic has evaluated 3,050 patients, with 1,250 participating in more than 100 clinical trials. Reflecting the newer realities of the AIDS epidemic, forty-two percent of the 984 patients currently being followed are people of color, and twenty-one percent are women.

# COLOPHON

The text was set in Bembo, a typeface designed
and modernized by the Monotype
Corporation in 1929 under the direction of
Stanley Morris. Bembo is based on Aldus
Manutius' typeface, De Aetna, originally cut for
the publication of Cardinal Bembo's *De Aetna*.
The display type is Trump Mediaeval, and the
folios are in Sabon Old Style.

Composed by Alabama Book Composition,
Deatsville, Alabama.

The book was printed by R R Donnelley,
Willard, Ohio and Reynosa, Mexico on acid
free paper.

# Genetics

## From DNA to Designer Dogs

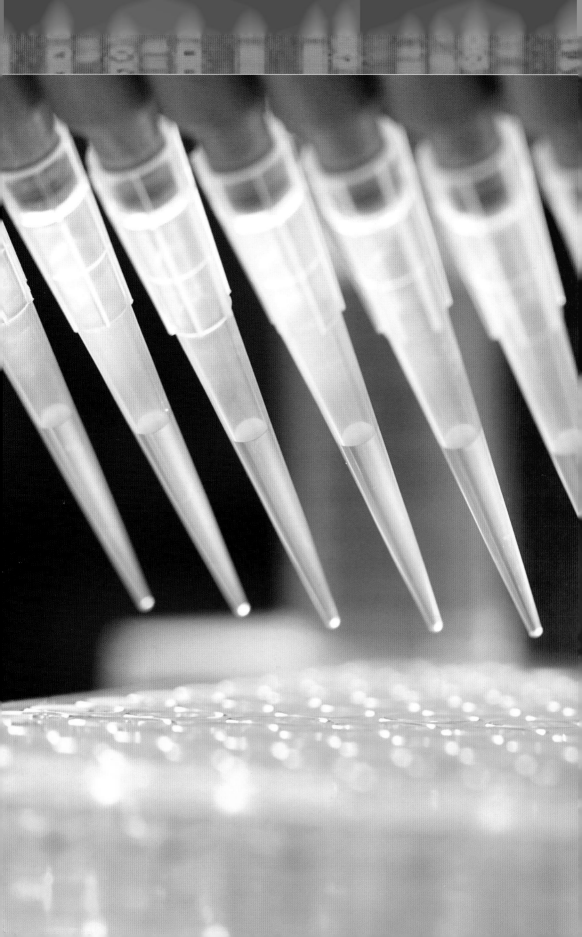

# Genetics

## From DNA to Designer Dogs

By Kathleen Simpson
Dr. Sarah Tishkoff, Consultant

NATIONAL
GEOGRAPHIC
Washington, D.C.

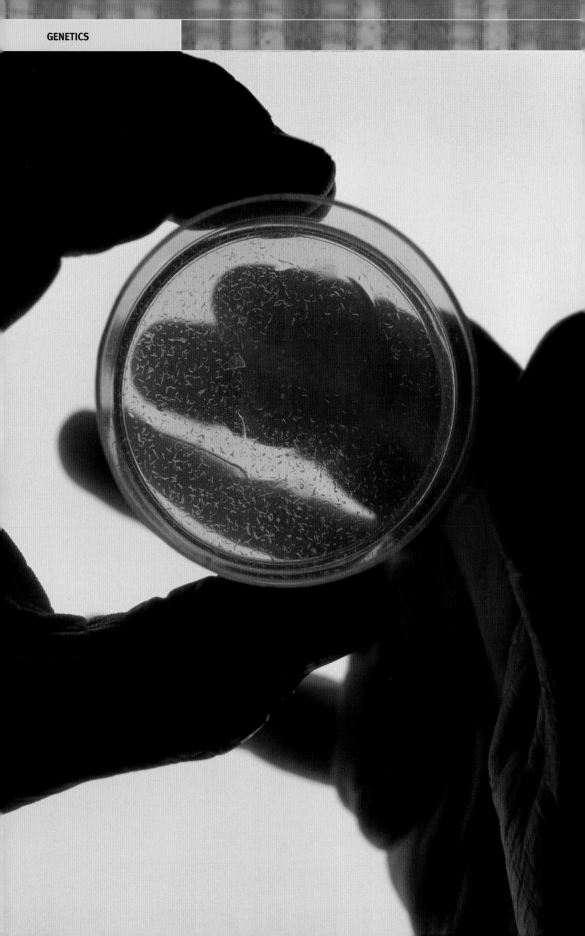

# Contents

Message From the Consultant 8

Mendel, the Father of Modern Genetics 9

Timeline of Genetic Research 10

## 1 Ancient DNA 12

Royal genes • Pharaoh gone missing • Historic discoveries • A mysterious mummy is found • Family tree, written in DNA • Problems with ancient DNA • Genetic science reveals the future as well as the past

## 2 Genetic Science 20

Green pollution fighters • Rabbit genes in trees • Slow cleanup in the most polluted places • A medium pizza with genetically modified canola oil • A problem or a solution?

## 3 Genes for Long Life 26

Very old worms • Why is my hair brown? • Switching genes on and off • Inherited traits • Two points of view

## 4 Fighting for Wildlife 32

Mysterious animal on the loose in Montana • Gathering gorilla DNA • Extracting DNA • New weapons • Meet a DNA investigator

< A *Caenorhabditis elegans* worm in a petri dish. The worm is ideal for genetic research because it is almost transparent, allowing scientists to more easily study its internal organs.

5

## 5 Microbial DNA 42

Why is microbial DNA important? • A map of microbial DNA • Scooping up life in the Sargasso Sea • The Human Genome Project • Microbial Genome Project

## 6 Genetics and Cloning 50

Ditteaux, the African wildcat • How does cloning work? • Cloning history • Problems of diversity • Why stop with African wildcats? • Growing a human heart

The Years Ahead 58

Glossary 59

Bibliography 60

On the Web 60

Further Reading 60

Index 61

About the Author and Consultant 63

Credits 64

< The mice on the middle and bottom layer of this tower were cloned from the animal on the top.

I first became interested in genetic research when I was an undergraduate student studying Anthropology at U.C. Berkeley. I wanted to use new scientific approaches to better understand questions such as, "When and where did modern humans evolve?" "What is the genetic basis of variable human traits such as height, skin color, and eye color?" In order to address these and other questions, I use anthropology, genetics, molecular biology, evolutionary biology, and computational biology. When I was a graduate student at Yale, I first discovered how much genetic diversity there is within and between African populations compared to populations from other regions in the world. This sparked my interest in studying African genetic diversity. For that reason, I have led research expeditions to Africa to collect DNA samples from thousands of individuals. From these samples, we have learned many interesting things about human evolution and African population history.

If you're reading this book, you must be intrigued by genetics, too. Perhaps your interest in the field will lead you to a career as rich and rewarding as mine has been so far.

*Dr. Sarah Tishkoff*
*University of Pennsylvania*

Λ **Dr. Sarah Tishkoff (center) makes frequent trips to Africa, where she does research.**

# Mendel, the Father of Modern Genetics

Mendel studied seven different traits in pea plants in order to understand how those traits are passed on from one generation to the next, or inherited:

1) flower color - purple or white

2) flower position - axial (side) or terminal (end)

3) stem length - long or short

4) seed shape - smooth or wrinkled

5) seed color - yellow or green

6) pod shape - inflated (puffy) or pinched (shrunken)

7) pod color - green or yellow

Trained in mathematics, Mendel learned how to design experiments and analyze information. His studies of garden peas lasted 8 years, and he observed more than 25,000 plants! The conclusions Mendel reached about the principles of heredity in plants apply to people and animals as well. The way heredity works is basically the same for all complex life forms. (For more about Mendel, see page 15.)

9

# TIMELINE OF
# Genetic Research

< 1850 – 1860s
Gregor Mendel investigates inherited traits in pea plants.

V 1953 · James Watson (left) and Francis Crick stand next to their model of a DNA molecule.

∧ 1879 · Observations of salamander eggs lead to the discovery of chromosomes, the biological structures where genes are located.

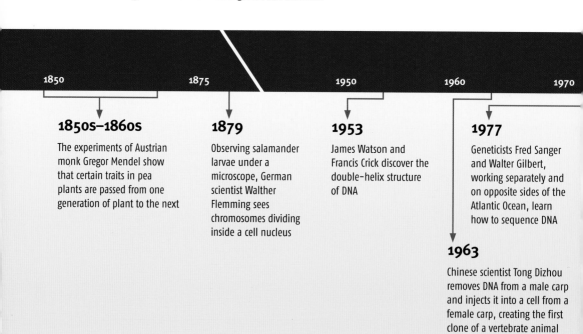

| 1850 | 1875 | 1950 | 1960 | 1970 |

## 1850s–1860s

The experiments of Austrian monk Gregor Mendel show that certain traits in pea plants are passed from one generation of plant to the next

## 1879

Observing salamander larvae under a microscope, German scientist Walther Flemming sees chromosomes dividing inside a cell nucleus

## 1953

James Watson and Francis Crick discover the double-helix structure of DNA

## 1977

Geneticists Fred Sanger and Walter Gilbert, working separately and on opposite sides of the Atlantic Ocean, learn how to sequence DNA

## 1963

Chinese scientist Tong Dizhou removes DNA from a male carp and injects it into a cell from a female carp, creating the first clone of a vertebrate animal

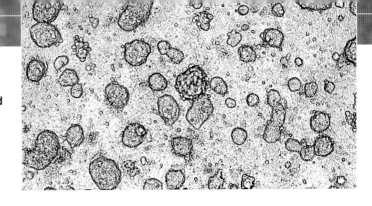

> **1998** · Embryonic stem cells hold great promise for treating and curing diseases in the future.

**V 1984** · British geneticist Alec Jeffreys

**V 1994** · The Flavrsavr tomato is the first engineered food approved for commercial distribution.

| 1980 | 1990 | 2000 |
|------|------|------|

## 1990

Doctors take white blood cells from a four-year-old girl with a disease that makes her body unable to fight off infections. They insert healthy genes into the white blood cells and put them back in the girl's body. The treatment is a success—the first successful gene therapy on a person.

## 1984

Alec Jeffreys develops DNA fingerprinting techniques that will be used around the world to solve crimes, identify people, and study animals

## 1994

A genetically engineered tomato—the Flavrsavr—is sold to the public for the first time. Flavrsavrs were made to stay fresh longer, and so, taste better. The U.S. government announced the tomato was safe to eat, but in the end, it proved too expensive to grow and market. Flavrsavrs are no longer sold.

## 2005

Using new, computerized tools that sort and sequence DNA quickly and precisely, the National Geographic Society and IBM launch a massive project to use DNA to map the migration of humans over the last 60,000 years

## 1998

U.S. scientists isolate human embryonic stem cells and use them to grow heart, blood, and bone cells

# Ancient DNA

## CHAPTER 1

## Royal Genes

**I**n the basement of the Egyptian Museum, a genetic researcher leans over an enormous female mummy. He observes the figure carefully. Dark skin stretches across the mummy's strong cheekbones and high, bald forehead. In the burial pose of ancient Egyptian noble and royal women, her arm lies folded across her chest, hand clenched in a tight fist, possibly to hold some sort of scepter, a staff symbolizing royal power.

The researcher works a long needle into the mummy's thigh, removing a sample of deoxyribonucleic acid (DNA) from her bone. The scientist then slips another needle into the same hole, but from a different angle, to collect another

◁ A photograph of the mummy of Queen Hatshepsut at the Egyptian Museum in Cairo, Egypt. The pharaoh's mummy was moved to Cairo from the Valley of the Kings in 2007, despite its first discovery in 1903.

sample. Researchers then whisk the 3,500-year-old tissue to the museum's new DNA laboratory, built for the sole purpose of studying ancient DNA. For their first major project, scientists are investigating whether the mummy is really Hatshepsut, Egypt's most powerful woman pharaoh—a king or queen of ancient Egypt.

## Pharaoh Gone Missing

Hatshepsut was a queen of Egypt in the 15th century B.C. When her husband, the pharaoh, died, Hatshepsut's stepson, Thutmose III, became king. Thutmose III was only a boy at the time, so his stepmother acted as regent—a sort of substitute king. The plan was that when Thutmose III grew up, he would take charge, but Hatshepsut had other ideas. Declaring herself pharaoh, she ruled Egypt with an iron hand for the next 22 years. In order to make herself seem more powerful in a country dominated by men, Hatshepsut behaved like a man. She wore men's clothing, called herself by male titles, and even wore the false beard that male pharaohs wore.

When Hatshepsut died, someone ordered her image and name erased from Egyptian art and writing, and even her mummy was lost. Many experts think her vengeful stepson, Thutmose III, was behind Hatshepsut's disappearance from history.

∇ Archaeologists believe this is the lost mummy of Queen Hatshepsut, the 15th century B.C. pharaoh of Egypt.

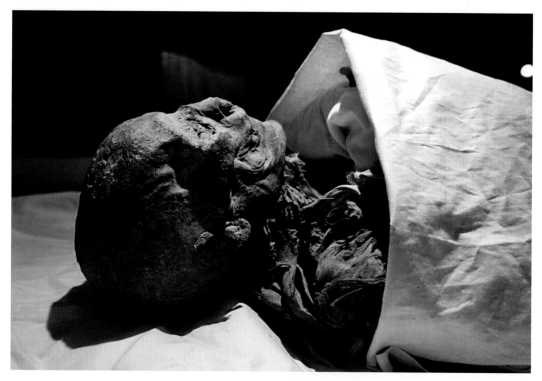

# Historic Discoveries

Modern genetic science is like an information volcano, exploding almost daily with new knowledge about the bodies of all living things. Early advances in genetic science happened more slowly.

An Austrian monk named Gregor Mendel (1822–1884) is often called the father of modern genetics. Working in the monastery garden, Mendel bred and crossbred thousands of pea plants and carefully recorded his experiments. He wanted to know how parent plants pass certain traits, like pod shape and flower color, to the next generation. He discovered predictable patterns in the way his pea plants inherited traits, and in 1866 he published his results for other scientists to read. At the time, few people paid attention to Mendel's experiments, but 30-some years later, around 1900, science rediscovered Mendel's work.

In 1908, a scientist named Thomas Hunt Morgan began breeding and studying fruit flies in his laboratory at Columbia University. In the famous "fly lab," Morgan and his students found that traits such as eye color are carried on specific chromosomes. The mother's chromosomes carry certain traits, while the father's chromosomes carry others. Morgan showed that genes line up on chromosomes, and their locations can be mapped. Today, genetic scientists still study Morgan's ideas about mapping the locations of genes.

In 1953, two scientists at England's University of Cambridge were trying to create three-dimensional cardboard models of DNA, the substance that seemed to determine how living things should grow and function. James Watson and Francis Crick knew they were close to discovering the structure of DNA, but their model was not quite right. Then Watson saw a vague x-ray image of DNA taken by a London scientist, Rosalind Franklin. The x-ray gave Watson's ideas a new direction, and he and Crick worked out the "double helix" (two spiral strands) structure of DNA. It was the biggest scientific discovery of the 20th century.

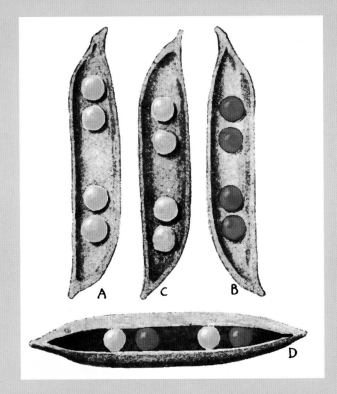

A historical drawing of the peas used by Gregor Mendel in his experiments on heredity.

∧ The Valley of the Kings in Luxor, Egypt, was first excavated in the 18th century, and work on the tombs found there continues today. Many of Egypt's greatest rulers were entombed in the valley from the 16th to the 11th century B.C.

## A Mysterious Mummy Is Found

In 1903, an English archaeologist named Howard Carter opened a tomb in Egypt that held two female mummies, one of them very large and posed like a member of a royal family. Because he was searching for a male pharaoh, Carter resealed the tomb with the mummies still inside. A few years later, the tomb was opened again and the smaller

> A monument of Queen Hatshepsut stands by her tomb in Luxor, Egypt.

mummy was removed, but the large mummy was left behind. Over time, people wondered who she might be: Was it possible that the woman left in the tomb was the missing pharaoh, Hatshepsut? In 1990, experts reopened the tomb to study the mummy, who wore a wooden mask of the type that might attach to a false beard.

Evidence began to pile up. Researchers found a wooden box in the tomb containing internal organs that they believed must have belonged to Hatshepsut. Ancient Egyptians believed that all parts of a dead ruler's body were sacred, so when they removed a pharaoh's liver and other organs during the process of mummification, they saved the organs. A special box holding the organs was placed in the tomb with the mummy. High-tech scanning equipment showed that the box containing Hatshepsut's organs also held a tooth. When scientists scanned the head of the large mummy, they found that she was missing a tooth and that the hole in her jawbone exactly matched the tooth found in the box.

Experts announced that this mummy was the lost pharaoh Hatshepsut, and they set out to prove it with DNA.

⋁ An x-ray of the mummy of Queen Hatshepsut indicates where the pharaoh had lost a tooth while she was alive. The tooth was found buried in the tomb with her internal organs.

⋁ Egypt's antiquities chief, Zahi Hawass, observes the mummy of Queen Hatshepsut (second, right) at the Egyptian Museum, where it is now undergoing DNA testing.

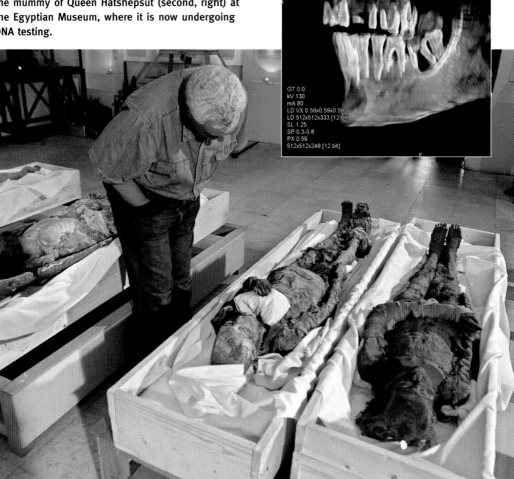

## Family Tree, Written in DNA

Your body is made up of cells, and each cell has a nucleus. In the nucleus, there are 46 chromosomes—23 from your mother and 23 from your father. These chromosomes are made up of a substance called DNA. DNA molecules are shaped like long spiral staircases, with a section of the staircase making up each gene. Genes carry instructions for how the body should grow, change, and work throughout its life.

Your family history can be traced through your DNA because you inherited genes from your parents and they inherited genes from their parents. Your DNA is similar to the DNA of your ancestors in very specific ways. In theory, Hatshepsut's DNA should show that she was related to other Egyptian royalty. In reality, proving anything with ancient DNA is complicated.

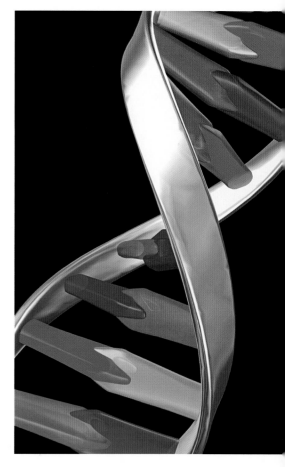

∧ A diagram of the structure of DNA

## Problems With Ancient DNA

Ancient DNA is fragile, so scientists have a hard time finding samples that are complete enough to study. Another problem is purity; people who find and study mummies leave some of their own DNA behind when they examine a body. They leave fingerprints or pieces of hair on the site, and it can be confused with the ancient DNA. To solve this problem,

< Parents pass traits to their offspring through chromosomes, allowing researchers to map a family tree through DNA.

scientists take DNA from places where it is likely to be pure, such as inside a mummy's bone.

The large mummy's DNA will have stories to tell. Experts have already identified the mummy of Hatshepsut's grandmother and collected DNA from it. If the large mummy is Hatshepsut, her DNA should look a lot like DNA from her grandmother. Early tests seem to show that she probably is the lost pharaoh, but testing of ancient DNA can take years to complete.

## Genetic Science Reveals the Future as Well as the Past

Scientists now know that an ancient and mysterious universe exists inside tiny cells. In 2005, a *Tyrannosaurus* bone found in Montana yielded proteins (organic compounds) that may be 68 million years old. These proteins look a lot like ostrich proteins, ·offering strong evidence that dinosaurs are related to modern birds. In 2007, researchers studying Greenland's ice cap found bits of DNA that were between 400,000 and 800,000 years old. The DNA came from insects and trees, showing that Greenland was once quite warm, and changed scientists' ideas about climate history. What other secrets will genetic scientists find, locked up inside cells?

Almost daily, genetic science uncovers new information about the past, and it reveals a few things about the future as well. In years to come, genetics will bring new, better ways to clean up pollution. Chapter 2 describes how scientists use genes to grow pollution-eating plants. Chapter 3 explains the traits that children inherit from their parents and how people can use genetics to be healthier and live longer. Chapter 4 shows how scientists use DNA to save endangered species from an uncertain future, and Chapter 5 discusses microbial DNA and how microbes affect our planet. Chapter 6 explains how DNA and cloning are used in today's world. Exploration is an important part of what makes us human. What better place to begin than inside our own cells?

< **Bones from a *Tyrannosaurus Rex* may hold clues to the creature's past.**

# Genetic Science

## CHAPTER 2

## Green Pollution Fighters

In 1986, a nuclear power plant in Chernobyl, Ukraine, exploded and burned, spewing radioactive material across the Northern Hemisphere. Even as firefighters fought the blaze, radioactive particles settled out of the sky onto rooftops, trees, soil, and waterways.

In the weeks, months, and years to follow, radioactive pollution became a huge problem near Chernobyl. The area was evacuated. Cleanup crews chopped down contaminated trees and buried them in concrete pits along with cars and tractors. A thick layer of soil was scraped up and buried, too. Amid

< Sunflowers were used as a natural method of ridding radioactive poisons from the ground after a nuclear accident in Chernobyl, Ukraine.

∧ Sunflowers float on rafts in a pond less than a mile (1.3 km) from the Chernobyl nuclear power plant in 1996.

the racket of bulldozers and trucks, one cleanup project was surprisingly quiet: Sunflower plants were floated in ponds on rafts. The rafts had slats in them to allow the plants' roots to grow through the water. The plants drew up radioactive poisons through their roots. The sunflowers left pond water 95 percent cleaner than it was after the accident.

When governments tested nuclear weapons in the 1940s, scientists monitored plants in areas where nuclear explosions took place. They wanted to study the effects of radiation (a by-product of nuclear reactions) on plants, and to learn how long those effects would last in soil and groundwater. These early experiments proved that plants draw radioactive pollutants out of the ground. Then, in the 1990s, researchers became interested in using plants to clean up polluted environments.

At first, some people thought the idea was far-fetched, but now, experts rely on plants to clean up pollution, even at some of the world's most polluted sites. Plants do the job for less money than it would cost to scrape up acres of dirt and haul it to a toxic waste dump. They leave the area looking nicer, too, but there is one problem: Plants work very slowly.

∨ The water-cooling facility at the Chernobyl nuclear power plant in 1986. Fallout from an explosion at the plant contaminated many parts of Europe, the Soviet Union, and some areas of North America.

## Rabbit Genes in Trees

Genetic scientists would like to make pollution-eating plants work faster. In laboratories at the University of Washington, Sharon Doty and her team may have found a way to do that. Dr. Doty takes genes from the livers of rabbits and inserts them into young poplar trees. All living things have genes that carry instructions for how cells should work. These instructions are different between animals and plants, but they are "written" in the same genetic code. So, in some cases, a plant can follow instructions from a mammal's gene. Both rabbits and poplar trees have genes that help them break down pollutants. Scientists already knew how to "turn up" the rabbit gene, to make it work faster. The transgenic trees (trees that scientists have genetically changed) eat pollution about 100 times faster than ordinary poplar trees do.

For now, Dr. Doty's trees are small, growing in glass jars in a laboratory. The team is looking for ways to alter the trees' own genes instead of adding genes from mammals. Doty thinks the trees will probably work even better that way. Researchers also want to make sure that the trees will not cause problems in the natural environment. Insects and other animals must be able to live in the trees and eat their bark, leaves, and roots without getting sick.

## Slow Cleanup in the Most Polluted Places

∧ Genetically altered trees are one way scientists are trying to combat pollution.

The U.S. government lists more than 1,200 places as Superfund sites—locations that are dangerously polluted and need to be cleaned up. At the Aberdeen Proving Ground in Maryland, 30 years of testing military weapons left poisonous chemicals behind in the soil and water. In 1990, the government added Aberdeen to its Superfund list. The cleanup has involved scraping away polluted soil, removing old storage tanks, and hauling off waste that lay above ground. In 1996, the government planted poplar trees (the old-fashioned kind, not transgenic trees) to draw pollutants out of the ground. The poplars draw up about 20 gallons (76 l) of polluted water from the soil each day (think about the gallon of milk in your refrigerator and multiply that amount by 20). Even at that rate, this cleanup could take 30 years to finish.

Another problem is making sure the trees do not spread into natural forests. Some people see transgenic trees as a possible threat, because no one really knows what would happen if they spread. In fact, the U.S. government has strict rules about using transgenic plants outside of laboratories. One reason Dr. Doty's team works with poplars is that they grow fast, but do not flower for several years. This means they could do their work and be cut down before they produce seeds and spread. The team hopes to try out the trees in a few superpolluted environments.

## A Medium Pizza With Genetically Modified Canola Oil

Insects can ruin a crop of corn. They burrow into the ears and stalks, feeding and tunneling until the corn is ruined, the leaves drop to the ground, and the stalks fall over in the wind. A whole season's worth of the farmer's work, time, and money is wasted. Genetic scientists wrestled with this problem and came up with an answer. They transferred genes from bacteria with natural insect-fighting abilities into the DNA of corn plants. The result was a corn plant that kills insects that feed on it, yet does not harm people who later eat the corn.

Since the 1990s, scientists have modified the genes in plants to suit the needs of people. Farmers have planted corn with built-in bug-killer, papayas that resist plant disease, and soybeans that are not harmed when a field is sprayed with weed-killer.

In the United States, genetically modified (GM) crops are so common that most people eat them every day in pizza, bread, cereal, or ice cream.

∧ **Insects known as corn borers can destroy entire crops. Geneticists have developed corn plants that poison the bugs that feed upon them.**

Most consumers do not even know when they are eating GM foods because they do not carry a label. For the most part, Americans do not eat fresh GM fruits and vegetables; instead, food manufacturers use GM crops to make packaged foods that consumers buy at the grocery store.

In the late 1990s, researchers developed a new strain of GM rice that was packed with vitamin A. They hoped the GM rice would help prevent blindness and other health problems caused by a lack of vitamin A. This could make a real difference in countries where rice is an important part of the people's diet.

## A Problem or a Solution?

Around the globe, many experts worry about how GM crops will affect the environment. They fear that pollen from insect-killing crops will blow onto nearby weeds, where butterflies and other creatures might eat it and die. They worry that the pollen from GM crops could be absorbed by weeds, creating "superweeds" that might take over an ecosystem. Some people also fear that these new foods may contain allergens, substances that cause allergic reactions.

Other people look forward to a day when genetically modified crops might solve many of the world's problems. Will a poor farmer on a sliver of land be able to grow enough GM food to feed a family? Will cancer patients fight their disease by eating vitamin-packed GM foods? Will GM foods that stay fresh longer and ship

∧ Much of Asia relies on rice to feed its citizens. Developing high-yield rice plants is one project geneticists are working on.

easily allow consumers to eat more fruits and vegetables? Whether GM plants are a problem or a solution, they are already part of our lives.

∨ Researchers grow genetically modified plants in their laboratories and hope the results they achieve translate to large-scale farming.

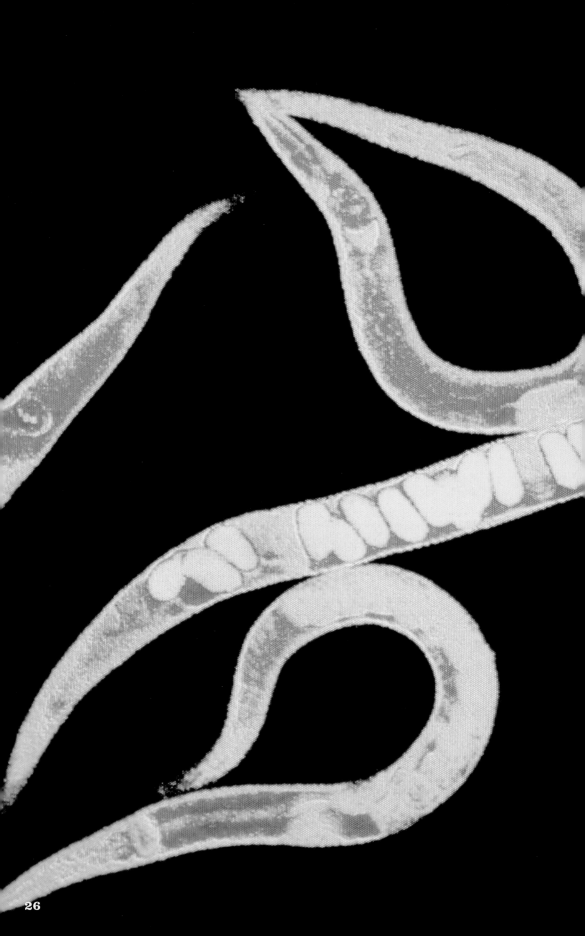

# Genes for Long Life

## Very Old Worms

**A**t two weeks of age, a worm known as *Caenorhabditis elegans* lies near death, its body shriveled and barely moving. This tiny roundworm is a senior citizen, as roundworms go. *C. elegans* normally lives two or three weeks, and it shows its age just as most people do. Its skin changes, its movements slow, and it does not chase food with the same energy it had as a youngster.

Under a nearby microscope lies a cousin that is five weeks old. This *C. elegans* squirms like a kindergartner, even though it is more than twice as old as the other one. Scientists have found the key to long life in roundworms: Genes that keep

< Scientists study the DNA of roundworms for insight into aging and the genetic mechanisms that control it.

*C. elegans* young. Using chemicals and diet to turn some genes off and make others work harder, researchers have learned how to keep the worms healthy and strong, right into old age. Could genes do the same for you? Cynthia Kenyon, a scientist at the University of California in San Francisco, thinks it might be possible.

> A 103-year-old resident of Sardinia, Italy, still enjoys good health. Scientists look to people like her to understand whether long life is a result of genetics or the environment people live in, or both.

∧ Researchers study the short life span of dogs compared to the average human life span in order to understand which genes control how our bodies age.

For a long time, scientists believed that our bodies wear out as we grow older, like a machine with worn-out parts. Dr. Kenyon wondered why some animals live much longer than others. Why does a Labrador retriever live just 10 or 15 years while humans can live into their 80s and beyond? Could it be that genes tell the body how long it should live?

## Why Is My Hair Brown?

Your genes determine whether you will have curly hair or straight, blue eyes or brown. Genes can even give you the ability to do things other people cannot, like wiggle your ears. These are inherited traits, traits you get from your mother, your father, or both.

Not all inherited traits are as obvious as hair and eye color, though. Genes can also influence the way you operate; athletic ability and musical talent are two examples. But this does not mean you can blame your parents if gym is the hardest class in your day or if you cannot sing like a rock star. Genes do not completely control your actions. Other factors, such as what foods you eat, where you live, and what you and your friends do for fun, also influence the ways your body's cells work. One of the trickiest jobs that genetic scientists have is figuring out how important genes are.

∧ Genes are not the only indication of an individual's potential for long life. A healthy lifestyle greatly influences how people will age.

## Switching Genes On and Off

Each gene has its own job to do. Some genes control how people see colors, while others tell hair how to grow. Dr. Kenyon's team searched for genes that affected aging. They found one that made the worms live longer—twice as long, in fact. Then they found another gene that was a sort of "master switch" for several genes, turning them off and on. By experimenting with these genes, researchers soon had worms living five and six times as long as "wild" worms would. The old worms were healthy and active, wriggling under the microscope.

# Inherited Traits

In Sardinia, an island in the Mediterranean Sea, a surprising number of residents are centenarians—people over a hundred years old. This is especially true among men. Scientists wonder why: Is the answer diet? A lifetime of hard work? Or does long life just "run in the family"? Scientists are still searching for answers to these questions.

You might be surprised at some traits that you can inherit from your parents:

- Does your hair form a small point in the middle of your forehead? That point is called a widow's peak. Does your mother or father have a widow's peak?

- Do you have a dimple, a small dent, in the center of your chin? Does anyone else in your family have a chin dimple?

- Can you distinguish between red and green? Red/green color blindness is often an inherited trait, although it can have other causes.

- Stick out your tongue and try to curl the sides of it upward. If you have brothers or sisters, see how many of them can do it.

- Take a look at the back of your hand. Each finger has three segments, or parts. Does hair grow on the middle segment of your fingers?

- Do the bottom of your earlobes attach directly to your head, or does the lobe hang free? What do your parents' earlobes look like?

∧ A Sardinian man, age 100. The high number of centenarians on this Italian island has led researchers to hypothesize that some people carry genes that code for a long life span.

Some of those genes that affect aging exist in human DNA, too, but it is quite a leap from tweaking the genes of a microscopic worm to extending the life of a human. Dr. Kenyon thinks science will make that leap, but only after years of hard work. Along the way, researchers may find other problems linked to genes. We already know that genes somehow influence many terrible diseases, including some types of cancer and mental illness. As scientists figure out which genes do what, they may be able to prevent some of the world's biggest health problems.

∧ Dr. Cynthia Kenyon hopes scientists can apply the information they have learned from studying roundworms to study human aging and longevity.

## Two Points of View

If you could be strong and healthy at the age of 120, would you want to live that long? Some people say no—a life that long would be tiresome. Besides, if everyone lived more than a century, the world might become awfully crowded. Would we run out of food, water, and space for all those people? Genetic scientists argue that medicine has already helped people live longer than they did in the past. The world is already crowded, and these researchers think that humanity will adapt to future changes just as it has adapted to so many in the past. Why not live longer, they ask, if the body and mind are strong?

∨ Crowds of people rush to work in Bombay, India, the fifth most populated city in the world. Overpopulation is an issue scientists who study genetics and aging must confront.

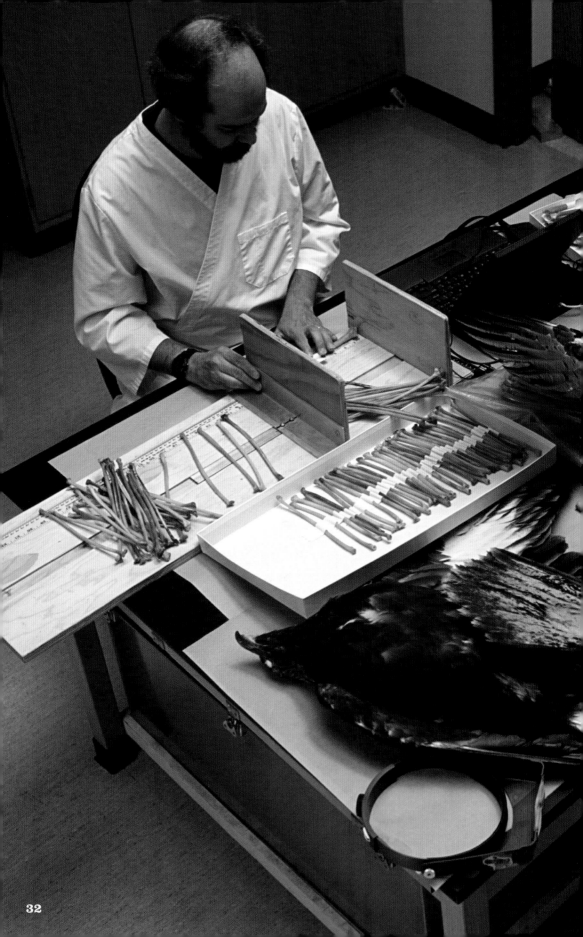

# Fighting for Wildlife

## CHAPTER 4

## Mysterious Animal on the Loose in Montana

**A** large package sits on the desk of DNA investigator Dyan Straughan. The package is wrapped in the special tape that investigators use to seal packages containing evidence. Straughan knows what it contains. Newspapers and radios have covered the story for weeks: Some kind of animal had slaughtered 120 sheep on ranches across Montana. Witnesses had seen the beast, but no one was sure what it was—a wolf? a dog? Whatever it was, the animal cost ranchers a lot of money, so they called the Montana Department of Fish, Wildlife, and Parks for help.

< Wildlife forensic scientist Pepper Trail, with the National Fish and Wildlife Forensics Laboratory in Ashland, Oregon, catalogs bones of bald eagles to create a database of eagle wing bone dimensions for use in future wildlife crime cases.

⋀ The pathology lab at the NFW Forensics Laboratory in Ashland, Oregon. Animal carcasses are laid out for study by scientists in order to identify the species.

The state then called the federal government, because federal law protects wolves. Federal agents, agreeing that the animal was a threat, finally found it and killed it, but they still were not sure what it was. So they sent its body to the National Fish and Wildlife Forensics Laboratory in Ashland, Oregon, where it ended up on Straughan's desk.

She opens the package and examines the carcass carefully. The animal's coloring is unusual—a little more yellow than is normal for a wolf. She uses a razor to slice off a tiny piece of its ear, about one-fourth the size of a pencil eraser. That tiny snippet of tissue will yield more than enough DNA to identify what type of animal killed the sheep. Genetic science is a powerful tool in the hands of investigators, helping them solve wildlife mysteries that would once have been unsolvable.

The Ashland laboratory, the most advanced wildlife forensics lab in the world, is dedicated to solving crimes against protected wildlife. Using DNA, investigators can tell exactly what species a sample comes from. They can, for example, analyze DNA from a shipment of leather shoes entering the country and compare it to the DNA of endangered caimans (a smaller cousin of an alligator). If the leather is made from the hide of a protected species, the shoes are confiscated and the seller pays a hefty fine. In a well-known Oregon case, investigators used DNA science to nab a merchant selling powder made from the horn of an endangered black rhinoceros. Most of the time, powders labeled as rhinoceros horn are really made from bones of other animals. By analyzing DNA in the powder, though, scientists learned that the Oregon merchant really did have in his shop a horn from a black rhinoceros. Just having the powder for sale is against the law.

Wildlife crime investigators can even link DNA evidence to a particular animal. When local residents report a possible poaching incident, investigators can analyze DNA samples collected from blood spots at the scene. They compare that DNA to meat found in a poacher's freezer or hides hanging on

∧ **Boots covered in skins can be analyzed to determine whether they are made from the hides of protected species.**

his wall. If both the sample and the meat or hide come from the same endangered antelope, the poacher may be arrested, tried, fined, or even jailed. Knowing that they could be punished may give some poachers second thoughts about killing protected wildlife.

> **Wildlife forensic scientists are charged with determining if products are made out of species protected by law, including caimans.**

# Gathering Gorilla DNA

∧ DNA fingerprinting helps researchers and conservationists protect the endangered lowland gorilla.

Elbowing through thick underbrush, researchers in Gabon, a country in Africa, keep sharp eyes out for snags of gorilla hair on tree limbs or fallen logs. They scour the rain forest for hair, dung, and nesting places of western lowland gorillas, an endangered ape. The samples will yield DNA fingerprints of individual gorillas, telling the scientists where they gather, which ones move together, and how they die.

Finding and studying gorillas in the dense jungle is difficult, so researchers have never really understood how western lowland gorilla groups live. DNA science is changing all that.

When scientists found the carcass of a dead silverback (male gorilla) in 1993, they collected hairs from the scene. They could tell that the silverback had died in a fight with another gorilla, but they did not know which one killed it or why. Years later, they analyzed the hairs from the carcass, along with other hairs and dung collected in the area. Using DNA fingerprinting, they learned that another silverback had been nearby that day. They also learned that a female gorilla had left with the other male. Scientists concluded that the silverbacks probably fought over her and the female left with the victor.

This silverback was killed in a fight, but western lowland gorillas face other threats as well, including disease, poaching, and loss of habitat. With knowledge gained through DNA, scientists, governments, and conservation groups are working together to save the western lowland gorilla from extinction.

## Extracting DNA

The first thing that DNA investigators do is find a usable tissue sample, such as blood, hide, hair, or bone. They dissolve the tissue and clean away anything that is not needed for testing, such as fat. Next, they do something called a PCR reaction to make copies of a section of DNA so that it is easier to examine. At this point, they may be able to identify the species, but not the particular animal. For that, investigators look for peculiarities in the DNA, chemical markers that are unique to one animal—a DNA fingerprint. To find out where the animal came from, they compare these results to the DNA of known groups, or populations, of animals in the same species. Scientists can consult animal DNA databases for mammals, birds, and other species to confirm their results.

∇ An image of a DNA fingerprint taken from an amplified section of DNA.

∇ A technician at the National Institutes of Health's Genomics Center works on DNA fingerprinting.

∧ **Illegal wildlife products are seized by customs officials and made available to wildlife forensic scientists, who investigate the origin of the products in order to stop the illegal activity.**

It can be a long, tedious job, because samples are often damaged or contaminated and do not always give reliable answers immediately. When this happens, the investigators keep working at it, sometimes for many months. A DNA fingerprint can provide a great deal of information—when investigators are able to decode it.

## New Weapons

When Dyan Straughan finishes testing the mysterious animal's DNA, her results are a surprise. The creature's DNA shows it is related to three separate groups of wolves:

a group in the Great Lakes region, a group in northern Canada and Alaska, and a third group that is found across North America. This combination would be almost unheard of in a wild wolf. Straughan concludes that the carcass in her lab probably belongs to a domesticated wolf or a wolf/dog hybrid, one that a breeder deliberately bred as a pet. The animal either ran away or was released, and it resorted to killing sheep in order to stay alive. The situation is a clear reminder that wild animals do not make good pets.

No pet owner has claimed the animal, possibly because the owner would have to pay for the dead livestock. Montana laws require owners of animals that are more than half wolf to register them with the state. They are also required to have wolf hybrids marked with a tattoo, but this animal has no tattoo and is not registered. No one is charged with a crime, but thanks to DNA science, the mystery has been solved.

Genetic science has changed the way criminal investigators and conservationists operate, bringing new weapons to the fight to save protected wildlife. Wildlife protection laws have been in place for a long time, but in the past, they were often difficult to enforce. Investigators relied on tire tracks, footprints, ballistics tests, and witnesses to link criminals to their crimes. These are all important tools, and investigators still use them today, but they are not always enough. Solid DNA evidence is often necessary to convict people who have committed crimes against wildlife.

Buying and selling products that come from protected wildlife has become a worldwide, billion-dollar business, despite the fact that it is illegal. In fact, illegal trade of horns, hide, and meat has seriously endangered some species. Wildlife forensics investigators like Dyan Straughan stay busy, searching for clues in animal DNA.

∧ Genetic fingerprinting has led to the identification of new species of wolves, in addition to helping experts solve crimes against protected species.

> **This researcher works at the NFW Forensics Laboratory, the only crime lab in the world devoted to protecting animals.**

# Meet a DNA Investigator

Dyan Straughan is a DNA investigator at the National Fish and Wildlife Forensics Laboratory in Ashland, Oregon. Straughan works mostly on wolves. Any investigator can work on any type of animal, but by focusing on only a few species, each person becomes something of an expert on those animals.

**◘ When people ask what kind of work you do, how do you describe your job?**

**◪** I work at the Animal Forensics Lab. The lab is just like a human crime lab, except that the victims are animals and not people. So if there is a poacher that kills a deer in a national park or a wildlife refuge, we can determine how it died—arrow, gunshot, poison—and match the gut pile found at the crime scene to a bloodstain on the suspect's knife and meat in the suspect's freezer. We do not answer questions like "does

this bird have West Nile [virus]" or "does this fish population have high levels of mercury." We only deal with crimes against animals, and, since we are a federal lab, we only deal with federal issues. We generally don't do poaching cases that deal with "out of season" issues or things like that. But, because we are a federal crime lab, we get cases from all across the country and the world. Since people often try to bring in animal products from other countries that are illegal, such as tiger products or primate products, those

items are sent to the lab for identification.

**◘ What part of your work is most exciting?**

**◪** Sometimes, people will try to smuggle meat or animal products into the United States from other countries. People want to have things that may remind them of a trip that they took, like a necklace made from a lion's tooth or a bracelet made from the shell of a sea turtle. And sometimes people try to smuggle in meat to eat that reminds them of their homeland, things like rats, monkeys, or duikers (a type of small African antelope). These cases are exciting for me. It's a real mystery to solve.

**◘ What animal [species] do you help [protect]?**

◙ Unfortunately, all of the animals I work with have already died, so I can't save them.... I hope that the work that I do will help people understand that we (society) have rules about what is OK to kill and what is not, and we have those rules so that years from now, our grandchildren and great-grandchildren will be able to go and see elephants in Africa, lynx, wolves, polar bears, zebras, sea turtles, and all the other animals that each have their place in the circle of life.

**◘ What qualifications would I need in order to do the work you do?**

◙ The minimum that one would need to do the work that I do is a bachelor's [degree] in biology. I have a master's degree in biology, with a focus in genetics. A Ph.D. is the best.

**◘ [That sounds like a lot of school.] Did you like school?**

◙ For me, the biology was not that difficult, nor was the genetics (even the math was OK). I am HORRIBLE with language skills, you know, what is a prepositional phrase, what

∧ Mounted specimens of Asian gazelles are kept in the NFW laboratory so scientists can collect hair, horn, and tissue samples to compare to DNA they are investigating.

is the correct placement of a comma or an apostrophe. And if it weren't for spell checkers on computers, no one could even figure out what it is I am trying to say. Overall, I was a pretty good student, and I liked school....

**◘ Is there a "DNA myth" that you would like to dispel?**

◙ You can't tell how old someone (or something) is with DNA—you start out with the same DNA sequence that you die with, age doesn't change it.

**◘ What changes do you expect to see in the field of genetics in your lifetime?**

◙ I know that the methods that I use will be pretty old-

school soon, but I do expect that we are well on the way to clearer understanding of the world around us, and that with the advances in technology, we can sequence the genomes of more and more species and use that information to figure out how processes in the cell and the body work.

**◘ Is there anything else you would like us to know?**

◙ Even if you don't think that you will ever use science or math or physics when you grow up, really, it's not so bad, it can be fun.

## CHAPTER 5

# Microbial DNA

## Why Is Microbial DNA Important?

In Yellowstone National Park, microbes thrive in water that stews at 150°F (66°C). Busily turning light into chemical energy, they grow in swirls of red, yellow, brown, and green. Could scientists learn to produce energy with the same efficiency that these microbes do?

In the polluted mud of Chesapeake Bay, other microbes "inhale" rust to produce energy, in the same way you breathe in oxygen to help you break down food to produce energy. In the process, the microbes change the rust to a solid form of iron that won't mix with water and is easy to remove. Scientists are investigating to see if the microbes

< The DNA of microbes in hot springs at Yellowstone National Park in Wyoming is studied in an effort to learn more about energy production.

can do the same thing with uranium. At a Colorado site where groundwater is polluted with uranium, the scientists feed the rust-breathing microbes, encouraging them to grow. The microbes flourish, and as they do, they change uranium to a solid form—one that won't mix with water.

Other microbes live around vents at the bottom of the ocean, where superheated chemicals leak into the sea. They live under pressure that would crush you, in darkness that would leave you confused, and eat hydrogen sulfide, a chemical that would poison you. They appear to have lived this way for billions of years, so scientists wonder if microbes like these can

∧ A technician works in a lab where thousands of strains of microbes are stored in deep-freeze refrigerators. Scientists are working on developing industrial products using living material rather than fossil fuels.

provide information about the beginnings of life on Earth. After all, microbes swarm all over the planet, outnumbering all other plants and animals combined.

∨ Samples of microbes are collected from the bottom of Great Salt Lake in Utah.

∧ The 115-foot (35-m) *Weatherbird II* carries a plankton tow to collect samples for study in the Sargasso Sea off Bermuda.

Around the world, scientists want to know more about microbes— living organisms so small you cannot see them without a microscope. To understand how microbes do all the work that they do, scientists need to study their DNA.

## A Map of Microbial DNA

Not long ago, the only method scientists had for studying microbes involved growing them in laboratories. Researchers grew one species at a time in glass dishes. If the microbe colony grew, they studied it under a microscope. But scientists also wanted to learn about species of microbes that refused to grow in laboratories.

In 2003, a team of scientists from the Institute for Biological Energy Alternatives (IBEA) and the Bermuda Biological Station for Research took a new approach: They scooped up water from the Sargasso

Sea in the North Atlantic and studied everything in it. In this way, they learned about thousands of microbes in seawater and, more importantly, how all the microbes work together.

## Scooping Up Life in the Sargasso Sea

The Sargasso Sea has long been considered a mysterious place. It is part of the Bermuda Triangle, where many ships have disappeared. Fifteenth-century sailors saw its broad mats of seaweed and were fooled into thinking that land was nearby. Even the wildlife there is mysterious: Young glass eels hatch and hide in the mats of seaweed, but no one has ever seen an adult eel there.

Unlike any other sea in the world, the Sargasso Sea is surrounded by powerful North Atlantic Ocean currents (bodies of water that move in a single, unified direction) instead of land. These

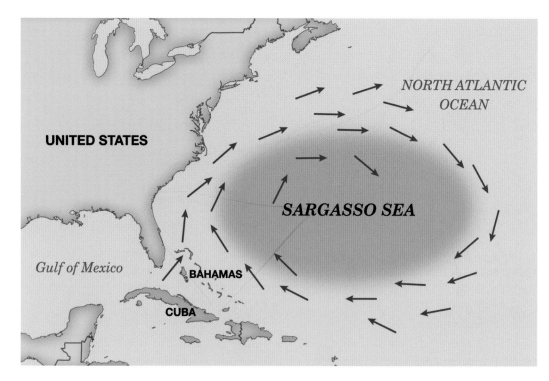

∧ The Sargasso Sea, in the North Atlantic Ocean, was long thought to be deserted of most organic life. Discoveries in 2007 showed that ocean currents bring nutrients to the region, allowing microscopic plants to thrive.

currents wrap around it like a belt, holding in the supersalty water. Scientists have studied the Sargasso Sea for decades, possibly more than any other part of the world's oceans. One reason the area was chosen for the 2003 study was that researchers expected to find a narrow range of microbe species. The water, they believed, held little food—not too many microbes for them to catalog in their experiments. It turns out they were wrong.

The IBEA researchers dredged up water samples from six research stations in the Sargasso Sea and poured the water through a series of paper filters. Each filter was finer than the one before it, so that smaller and smaller microbes got stuck on the filter paper. The researchers froze the filters and shipped them to Maryland, where other team members used chemicals to clean everything off the paper except DNA from the captured microbes. Then they used high-powered computers and specialized equipment to break apart and sort out thousands of different types of microbial DNA. In the final stage of the project, they set out to make "maps" of the microbe genomes.

A genome is the hereditary information of a cell encoded in the DNA. Every species of plant, animal, and microbe has its own unique genome. The human genome is different from the genome of a giraffe, or a lemon tree, or a microbe. To map the microbe genomes, the IBEA team determined the nucleotide sequence of DNA.

Incredibly, the water of the Sargasso Sea was teeming with microbes. The researchers discovered DNA for 1,800 new species, including more than a million genes that had never been studied before.

Since the Sargasso Sea project, scientists have scrambled to learn more about microbial DNA. The IBEA researchers have begun a long-term project called the Sorcerer II Expedition to sample seawater in oceans around Earth. Traveling on the *Sorcerer II,* a sailboat equipped

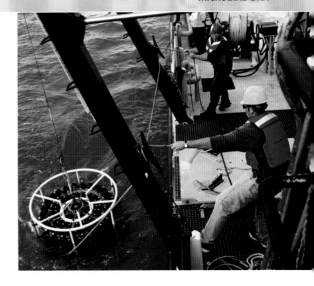

∧ A crew member of the *Weatherbird II* hauls in water samples containing microbes for study.

as a research vessel, they take 53-gallon (200 l) samples every 200 miles (322 km). Just as they did on the first project, they strain their samples through paper filters, freeze them, and ship them to a U.S. laboratory, where another team studies the DNA.

∨ Scientists from the *Sorcerer II* Expedition take water samples from an inland stream in Mexico, looking for microbes they will filter out and freeze for further study.

# The Human Genome Project

So what about your genome? How are you different from a microbe? For one thing, you are much more complicated. Your DNA is shaped like a tiny spiral staircase, with every step made up of two base chemicals. That staircase has about three billion steps! If the staircase was broken up into floors (first floor, second floor, etc.), each floor might represent a gene.

Human DNA has between 20,000 and 25,000 genes. We know this because thousands of scientists around the world worked together for 13 years, between 1990 and 2003, to make a record of human DNA. This huge project was called the Human Genome Project.

Your 20,000 genes are almost identical to those of other humans—very small differences make each person unique. By studying similarities and differences between people's genes, scientists are able to work out what individual genes do. It is an important task that will keep researchers busy for many years.

∧ **A bacterium housed inside cells in an insect has been shown to have the fewest number of genes in any known life-form, less than half of what scientists believed an organism needed to live.**

Microbes live in the sea, in soil, in food, and inside the human body. People often think of microbes as troublesome "bugs" that invade the body and cause infection or disease, but that is not the whole story. Most microbes do not make people sick; in fact, their activity supports the air we breathe and the atmosphere that protects the planet. By studying microbial DNA, scientists hope to learn how to do things that microbes do naturally, like harvesting energy efficiently and removing poisons from soil and water. Microbe DNA may also provide new medicines and ways to manage carbon dioxide, a contributor to climate change. Because microbes have existed far longer than humans—about 3.8 billion years—they may even help scientists learn how life on Earth began.

## Microbial Genome Project

Recent discoveries like the ones made by the IBEA researchers have piqued scientific curiosity about microbes. A massive project to research microbes, much like the Human Genome Project, has gotten underway—it is known as the Microbial Genome Project. With this project, scientists investigate not only individual microbes, but entire microbe communities. They want to know how individual genes help many species of microbes work together to solve problems, such as finding food in a polluted environment. Studies are being launched to investigate microbes in groundwater, in sewage, and even inside the human body. Early results show that microbes are far more important to humans than scientists once believed.

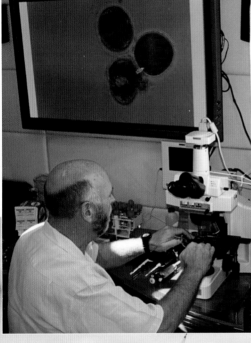

∇ Dr. J. Craig Venter, a scientist aboard the *Sorcerer II,* peers through a microscope at microbes found in water samples.

∇ The *Sorcerer II* will circumnavigate the globe under sail to study microbial populations in both the sea and on land.

# Genetics & Cloning

## CHAPTER 6

## Ditteaux, the African Wildcat

Ditteaux (pronounced ditto) looks a lot like an ordinary house cat. His coat is mostly gray with black stripes swirling across his back, and the fur of his belly is soft and white. Ditteaux may look tame, but, in fact, he is an endangered African wildcat. He lives in New Orleans, at the Audubon Center for Research of Endangered Species.

Ditteaux is also a clone. That means he is a genetic copy of his father, an African wildcat named Jazz. Scientists at the center think that cloning could be an important tool to use in saving some of Earth's most endangered animals.

< There is great hope that the endangered African wildcat population will be rescued by mating cloned male and female animals with each other.

## How Does Cloning Work?

Here's how Ditteaux came to be. First, scientists took DNA from cells belonging to Jazz, an African wildcat that was born at the Audubon Center. Then they removed an egg cell from a female house cat. They took out the DNA from the egg's nucleus and substituted Jazz's DNA. Next, they applied a small amount of electricity to the nucleus, so the DNA would bond to it and divide, becoming an embryo (an embryo is the first stage of life). Finally, the scientists returned the cloned embryo to the house cat's body, where it grew into a kitten—a kitten with the DNA of an African wildcat.

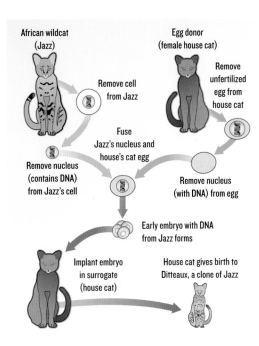

African wildcat (Jazz)

Egg donor (female house cat)

Remove cell from Jazz

Remove unfertilized egg from house cat

Fuse Jazz's nucleus and house's cat egg

Remove nucleus (contains DNA) from Jazz's cell

Remove nucleus (with DNA) from egg

Early embryo with DNA from Jazz forms

Implant embryo in surrogate (house cat)

House cat gives birth to Ditteaux, a clone of Jazz

∧ A cloned animal is the result of fusing cells from different specimens and embedding the resulting embryo in a surrogate.

# Cloning History

Cloning is not a new idea; gardeners have been cloning plants for centuries. Every gardener who takes a cutting from a plant and shoves it into the ground to grow roots is creating a clone of the original plant. Cloning of animals is more complicated, but has been going on for five decades.

▓ As early as 1952, a team of scientists in a Philadelphia laboratory cloned tadpoles.

▓ In 1996, Scottish researchers cloned a sheep and named her Dolly, after country singer Dolly Parton.

▓ In 1998, researchers in Honolulu used cloning methods to produce more than 50 mice that were genetically identical.

▓ Noah, a cloned gaur, was born in 2001 in Massachusetts. Nearly extinct, the gaur, found in Asia, is much like an ox. Noah died before he was two days old, but his owners say his death had nothing to do with the fact that he was a clone.

▓ In the 21st century, ranchers clone prize dairy cows, sheep, and other livestock. The process is expensive, so clones are used mainly for breeding.

Born in 2003, Ditteaux seems to be healthy, and behaves much like other African wildcats. In fact, he has fathered two sets of kittens whose mothers are also African wildcat clones (their DNA is different from Ditteaux's). The kittens themselves are not clones, but were conceived naturally. Dr. Betsy Dresser, director of the Audubon Center for Research of Endangered Species, seems excited about where this science could lead.

## Problems of Diversity

One of the biggest problems facing endangered species involves a lack of genetic diversity. This means that most of the remaining animals in a species have genes that are too similar. Genetic problems are passed

< Kittens born to African wildcat clones at the Audubon Center for Research of Endangered Species in New Orleans

from one generation to the next, and spread throughout the species. When this happens, a species can suffer because of inherited weaknesses: a weak immune system or a genetic disease. Cheetahs are a good example.

At one time, cheetahs roamed over much of the planet—in North America, Asia, Europe, and Africa. Around ten thousand years ago, something happened to kill most of Earth's cheetahs—possibly fewer than ten survived. No one is certain what killed off the cheetahs (it may have been more than one event), but other species died out at about the same time, too.

Over time, though, cheetahs bred and gave birth, and the world's cheetah population grew. Scientists know this is true because of genetics; testing of cheetah

∧ The cheetah population is at risk due to a lack of genetic diversity, making all cheetahs susceptible to the same health threats.

DNA shows that all the world's cheetahs come from a handful of distant ancestors. Genetically, they are all almost identical.

This means that they are all vulnerable to the same threats, such as disease or a change in habitat or climate. If one cheetah is affected by one of these threats, the whole species is likely to be affected. It is a dangerous situation for the world's cheetahs.

There is little scientists can do about the cheetahs' genetic problems, but they can try to make sure that other endangered species remain genetically diverse. For example, zoos can make sure that breeding animals are not related to each other. Governments can set aside areas for animal habitat, large enough to support genetically diverse groups of animals and plants. Cloning may become another part of the answer.

If an older animal of an endangered species lives in a zoo, an animal not closely related to wild populations, scientists can clone that animal. If the clone is allowed to breed with wild animals, the group becomes more genetically diverse. Here, though, is the really interesting part: Even if the animal in the zoo dies, scientists can freeze its DNA to use later.

## Why Stop With African Wildcats?

In a dozen or so "frozen zoos" around the world, DNA from endangered animals sits on shelves in special freezers. Gorillas, antelopes, elephants, bears, and many other species are part of the collection. Scientists believe they can keep the DNA frozen indefinitely until, some day in the future, it can be used to save species that are dying out.

This does not mean you can stop worrying about the giant panda and the elephant. Some species are harder to clone than others, and for some, cloning may never be possible. Also, saving endangered animals will not do any good if they do not have the habitat they need, so it is important to preserve the animals' habitats, too.

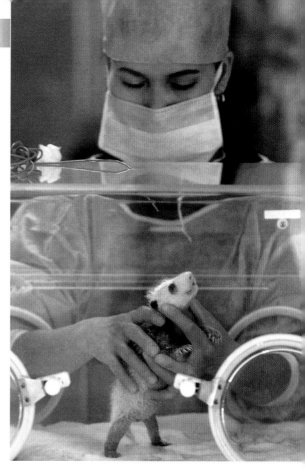

∧ A 16-day-old giant panda is held in its incubator at the Panda Breeding Research Base in Chengdu, China.

∨ A scientist at the Natural History Museum in London, England, observes a Polynesian tree snail. DNA from the snail and other endangered species will be frozen and preserved in an effort to safeguard the survival of animals that otherwise would be expected to go extinct within the next few decades.

Not all experts agree that cloning should be used this way. Some think that cloning science takes away money and time that should be spent on preserving animal habitats. Others point out that Ditteaux's embryo was carried in the body of a house cat. No one is completely certain of how the house cat's body may have affected the growing embryo. These experts caution that it is impossible to know what might happen if the DNA of clones like Ditteaux is mixed into wild populations.

## Growing a Human Heart

Creation of human clones does not interest serious scientists, but the use of cloned embryos to grow human cells is another matter. Blood, brain, heart tissue—all these body parts can be injured or become sick, and scientists would like to know how to grow new cells to replace them.

∧ **The Chinese government has unsuccessfully attempted to clone giant pandas. Scientists do not yet understand why some species are easier to clone than others.**

Embryos contain a special type of cell known as embryonic stem cells. Most cells in the body have a specific job to do, but embryonic stem cells are different. They don't yet have specific jobs. These cells have the amazing ability to transform themselves into any type of cell in the body. They can grow into tissue for the heart, skin, or even brain. Not all stem cells come from embryos, though.

Take a look in the mirror. Right there, in the skin on your face, busy adult stem cells are already doing what scientists would like to do. They transform into new tissue to

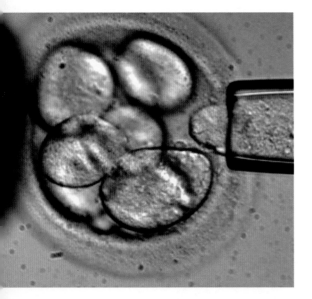

< **A single cell is removed from a human embryo to be used in growing stem cells for scientific research. Stem cell research is a rapidly advancing field of genetic research.**

replace the dead skin that flaked away last night in your sleep. In your brain, the same thing is happening, and in your heart, too; throughout many parts of your body, adult stem cells grow into new tissue to keep you going.

Adult stem cells are different from embryonic stem cells, though. Each adult stem cell seems to have its own list of jobs that it can do. Stem cells in skin transform into cells that the skin needs, stem cells in the brain transform into cells that the brain needs, and so on.

In 2007, something remarkable happened. Two teams of scientists, working in Japan and Wisconsin, announced that they had found genes that made adult stem cells in skin behave like embryonic stem cells. These cells were able to grow and change into other types of tissue.

Scientists have already learned how to slip stem cells out of the body, cause them to grow and reproduce, and make them transform into a different type of cell. The challenge now is to learn how to take stem cells from a sick or injured person, grow healthy new cells needed by that person's body, and then inject them into damaged tissue. There, these cells might do the work of rebuilding a weak heart or re-growing skin after a serious burn.

Scientists are still a long way from being able to grow body parts from stem cells, and some complicated problems stand in the way. The science is challenging enough, but questions about right and wrong may be even more difficult to answer. Many people feel it's wrong to experiment with embryonic stem cells, because embryos have to be destroyed in the process. These people feel that destroying an embryo means taking a life. Others argue that curing or preventing serious health threats like cancer and brain injury would save many, many lives.

Λ Junying Yu, a scientist at the University of Wisconsin-Madison Primate Research Center and the Genome Center of Wisconsin, is a leading researcher in stem-cell technology.

# The Years Ahead

∧ A Labradoodle named Wesley has a cream-colored coat like a Labrador that has the non-shedding characteristics of a poodle.

Genetic science sometimes moves in strange directions. The appeal of "designer dogs" is a perfect example. Dog breeders know that each breed has its own traits; for example, Labrador retrievers are playful and loving, and poodles do not shed hair. Breeders therefore crossbreed the two, hoping to produce a playful, loving dog that does not shed. But genetic scientists warn that the desirable traits do not always appear in the offspring. If they did, we would all be beautiful, intelligent, and talented.

Genetic scientists face difficult questions every time they collect a tissue sample, but these questions affect all of us. Where will genetic science take us, and how careful should we be about going there? What do you think?

# Glossary

**adaptation** — random changes (mutations) in DNA that enable animals to survive longer and have more offspring in certain environments

**adult stem cells** — cells found throughout the body that are able to become one of a number of cell types

**ancestors** — people from whom a person is descended; parents, grandparents, great-grandparents, etc.

**cell** — the smallest unit of life

**chromosome** — the part of a cell that contains genes

**circumnavigate** — to proceed completely around

**clone** — a genetic copy

**contaminate** — to make something impure

**DNA (deoxyribonucleic acid)** — a chemical that carries genetic instructions for how the body should grow and function

**DNA fingerprint** — a description of the pattern of genes in a person or animal's DNA

**ecosystem** — a community of organisms and their environment that functions as an ecological unit

**embryo** — the earliest stage of development for a living animal

**embryonic stem cells** — cells found in an embryo that are able to become any cell type in the body

**gene** — a section of the DNA strand; a carrier of traits that may be inherited by offspring

**gene therapy** — the altering of genes in order to affect their function

**genetic science** — the study of hereditary characteristics

**genetically modified crops** — food plants whose genes have been changed by scientists

**genome** — a record, or map, of the order of all the chemicals that make up a strand of DNA for one species

**habitat** — the landscape and area that an animal or plant needs in order to live

**hybrid** — the offspring of two animals or plants of different breeds

**mammal** — an animal that is warm-blooded, gives birth to live offspring, produces milk to feed its young, and (usually) has hair

**nucleus** — the part of a cell that controls how it functions, sometimes known as the "brain" of the cell

**organic** — characteristic of living organisms

**radioactive** — giving off energy in the form of waves or particles that are harmful to humans

**surrogate** — a living host who conceives or carries an embryo

**tissue** — a group of cells locked together to form the structural material of a plant or animal

**traits** — characteristics

**transgenic** — carrying a gene that has been transferred from a different type of plant or animal

## Bibliography

### Books

Ridley, Matt. *Genome: The Autobiography of a Species in 23 Chapters.* New York: HarperCollins, 2000.

### Articles

Kahn, Jennifer. *Mending Broken Hearts.* NATIONAL GEOGRAPHIC (February 2007): 40-65.

American Museum of Natural History. "Genomic Revolution." http://www.amnh.org/exhibitions/genomics/0_home/index.html (accessed May 22, 2008).

NATIONAL GEOGRAPHIC. "Food—How Altered?" May 2002. http://science.nationalgeographic.com/science/health-and-human-body/human-body/food-altered.html?nav=FEATURES (accessed May 22, 2008).

New Scientist. "Timeline: Genetics." September 4, 2006. http://www.newscientist.com/channel/life/genetics/dn9966-timeline-genetics.html;jsessionid=JAGIJHOIIFPN (accessed May 22, 2008).

PBS Nova. "Mummies 101." October 2000. http://www.pbs.org/wgbh/nova/chinamum/mummies101.html (accessed May 22, 2008).

## On the Web

American Museum of Natural History http://www.amnh.org/ology/genetics/

Audubon Nature Institute http://www.auduboninstitute.org

Discovery Channel, "Secrets of a Lost Queen" http://dsc.discovery.com/convergence/quest/lost-queen/program/program.html

National Geographic, "The Genographic Project" https://www3.nationalgeographic.com/genographic/

National Geographic Kids, "Trapped in Amber" http://www.nationalgeographic.com/ngkids/9609/amber/

PBS Nova, "Living at Extremes" http://www.pbs.org/wgbh/nova/abyss/life/extremes.html

Thinkquest Gene School http://library.thinkquest.org/28599/fundamentals.shtml

U.S. Fish and Wildlife Service http://www.lab.fws.gov/

## Further Reading

*Double Helix: The Quest to Uncover the Structure of DNA* (Science Quest). Washington, D.C.: National Geographic Society, 2006.

*Genetics: A Living Blueprint.* Minneapolis: Compass Point Books, 2006.

# Index

**Boldface** indicates illustrations.

Aberdeen Proving Ground, Md.
    23
Adult stem cells 56–57, 59
African wildcats
    cloning 51–53, 56
    kittens 52, **52,** 53
Aging 27–31
Ancestors
    definition 59
    family history 18
Ancient DNA 13–19
Asian gazelles **41**
Audubon Center for Research
    of Endangered Species, New
    Orleans, La. 51, 52, 53

Bacteria 24, 48
Bermuda Triangle 45
Black rhinoceroses 35
Boots, leather **35**

Caenorhabditis elegans **4,** 27–28
Caimans 35, **35**
Cairo Museum, Cairo, Egypt 13
Carp, cloned 10
Carter, Howard 16
Cats
    African wildcats **50–51,**
        51–53, **52,** 56
    cheetahs 53–54, **54**
    house cats 51, 52, 56
Cells
    definition 59
    nucleus 10, 18, 52, 59
    see also Stem cells
Centenarians **28,** 30, **30**
Cheetahs 53–54, **54**
Chernobyl, Ukraine: nuclear
    power plant 21–22, **22**
Chesapeake Bay 43
Chromosomes
    definition 59
    discovery of 10
    traits carried by 15, 18
Climate change 19, 48, 54
Clones and cloning
    African wildcats 51–53, 56
    definition 59
    dogs 58, **58**
    endangered species 51, 54, 55
    history 10, 53
    mice **6,** 53
Corn borers **24**

Crick, Francis 10, **10,** 15
Crime solving 11, 33, 35, 39, 40
Crossbreeding 15, 58

Dinosaurs 19, **19**
Ditteaux (African wildcat) 51,
    52, 53, 56
Diversity, genetic 53, 54
DNA (deoxyribonucleic acid)
    ancient DNA 13–19
    definition 59
    diagram of structure **18**
    discovery of structure 10, 15
    extracting 37–38
    fluid samples **2–3**
    microbial DNA 19, 45–49
    models **10,** 15
    sequencing 10, 11
    see also Genes
DNA fingerprints
    animal identification 36,
        37–38
    chemical markers 37
    definition 59
    image **37**
Dogs
    clones 58, **58**
    crossbreeding 58
    Labradoodle puppy **1**
    life span 28, 29
    wolf-dog hybrids 38–39
    see also Wolves
Doty, Sharon 23, 24
Double helix 10, **10,** 15
Dresser, Betsy 53

Ecosystems 25, 59
Egyptian Museum, Cairo, Egypt:
    mummies **12–13, 17**
Embryonic stem cells 11, **11,** 56,
    57, 59
Embryos
    African wildcats 52, 56
    cloning 52, 56
    definition 59
    human embryo **56**
    see also Embryonic stem cells
Endangered species
    cloning 51, 54, 55
    illegal wildlife products 35, 39
    problems of diversity 53–54
    see also African wildcats;
        Western lowland gorillas

Family history 18
Flavrsavr tomato 11, **11**
Flemming, Walther 10
Food, genetically engineered 11,

    11, 24–25, 59
Franklin, Rosalind 15
Fruit flies 15

Gaur, cloned 53
Gene therapy
    definition 59
    first successful 11
Genes
    aging and 27–31
    definition 59
    location 10, 15, 59
Genetic research, timeline of
    10–11
Genetic science
    definition 59
    future of 19, 58
    historic discoveries 15
Genetically modified (GM) crops
    24–25, 59
Genomes 41, 46–49, 59
Giant pandas 55, **55, 56**
Gilbert, Walter 10
Glossary 59
Gorillas 36, **36,** 55
Greenland
    climate history 19
    ice cap 19

Hatshepsut, Queen (Egypt)
    DNA testing 17, 18, 19
    monument **16**
    mummy **12–13,** 14, 16–17, **17**
    rule 14
Hawass, Zahi **17**
Heart tissue 56
Human Genome Project 48, 49
Humans
    embryo **56**
    life span 28, 29, 30, 31
    number of genes 48
Hybrids
    definition 59
    wolf-dog hybrids 38–39

Insects
    bacterium in cells 48
    butterflies 25
    corn borers **24**
    destruction of crops 24
    DNA from 19
    fruit flies 15
    transgenic trees and 23
J
Jazz (African wildcat) 51, 52
Jeffreys, Alec 11, **11**
K
Kenyon, Cynthia 28–29, **31**

Kittens 52, **52,** 53

Labrador retrievers 29, 58, 64
Life spans 27, 28, 29, 30

Mammals
    definition 59
    DNA databases 37
    genes 23
Mendel, Gregor 10, **10,** 15
Mice, cloned **6,** 53
Microbes 19, 43–49
Microbial Genome Project 49
Migrations, human 11
Molecules: DNA molecule 10,
    **10,** 18
Montana
    sheep killings 33–34
    tyrannosaurus bone 19
    wolf hybrids 39
Morgan, Thomas Hunt 15
Mummies **12–13,** 13–14, **14,** 16,
    **17,** 18–19

NFW Forensics Laboratory,
    Ashland, Oregon **32–33, 34,**
    34–35, **39,** 40
Nuclear weapons 22
Nucleus
    chromosomes 10, 18
    cloning 52
    definition 59

Ocean currents 45–46
Overpopulation 31

Pandas, giant 55, **55, 56**
Pea plants 10, 15, **15**
Pharaohs 13, 14, 16, 17
    see also Hatshepsut, Queen
Plants
    cloning 53
    corn plants 24, **24**
    genetically modified plants
        24–25, **25**

pea plants 10, 15, **15**
pollution-fighting plants 19,
    21–24
poplar trees 23, **23,** 24
sunflowers **20–21,** 22, **22**
Poaching 35, 36, 40
Pollution, cleaning up 19, 21–24
Polynesian tree snail **54**
Poodles 58, 64
Poplar trees 23, **23,** 24

Rabbit genes 23
Radioactive particles 21, 59
Rhinoceros horn 35
Rice 24, **25**
Roundworms **4, 26–27,** 27–28
Rust-breathing microbes 43–44

Salamanders 10, **10**
Sanger, Fred 10
Sardinia, Italy: centenarians **28,**
    30, **30**
Sargasso Sea
    glass eels 45
    map 46
    microbial research 45–47
    ocean currents 45–46
    research vessel **45**
    seaweed 45
Sheep, cloned 53
Sorcerer II (research vessel) 47,
    **49**
Stem cells 11, **11,** 56–57, 59
Straughan, Dyan 33, 38, 39, **40**
Sunflowers **20–21,** 22, **22**
Superfund sites 23

Tadpoles, cloned 53
Thutmose III, King (Egypt) 14
Timeline of genetic research
    10–11
Tomato, genetically engineered
    11, **11**
Tong Dizhou 10
Trail, Pepper **32–33**

Traits
    of breeds of dogs 58, 64
    definition 59
    inherited 29, 30
    pea-plant experiments 10, 15
    role of chromosomes 15, 18
Transgenic: definition 59
Transgenic trees 23–24
Triplets **63**
Tyrannosaurus bones 19, **19**

Uranium 44

Valley of the Kings, Luxor,
    Egypt 13, **16**
Ventner, J. Craig **49**

Watson, James 10, **10,** 15
Weatherbird II (research vessel)
    **46, 47**
Western lowland gorillas 36, **36**
White blood cells 11
Wildlife products, illegal 35, **38,**
    39, 40–41
Wolves 38, **39**
    forensic investigations 34,
        38, 40
    genetic fingerprinting 39
    new species 39
    protection of 34
    wolf-dog hybrids 38–39
Worms **4, 26–27,** 27–28, 29, 31

X-ray images
    DNA 16
    mummy **17**

Yellowstone National Park,
    Wyo.: hot springs **42–43**

Zoos 54

## About the Author

Kathleen Simpson lives in the hill country of central Texas with her two children, husband, and dogs. She has authored five books for young people. In addition to *National Geographic Investigates Genetics,* she has also written *National Geographic Investigates Extreme Weather* for the Society.

## Consultant

Sarah Tishkoff did her undergraduate studies in Anthropology and Genetics at U.C. Berkeley. She received her Ph.D. in Human Genetics from Yale University in 1996 and did postdoctoral research in human population genetics at the University of the Witwatersrand in Johannesburg, South Africa, and at Pennsylvania State University from 1997 to 2000. She was an Assistant Professor of Biology at University of Maryland from 2000 to 2007 and is currently an Associate Professor of Genetics and Biology at the University of Pennsylvania. Dr. Tishkoff is a recipient of an NSF Sloan postdoctoral fellowship in Molecular Evolution as well as Burroughs Wellcome Fund and David and Lucile Packard Foundation career awards. Her laboratory studies patterns of genetic diversity in African populations, human evolutionary history, and the genetic basis of resistance to infectious disease.

∧ Triplets share the exact same DNA because they all originated from the same fertilized egg.

Founded in 1888, the National Geographic Society is one of the largest nonprofit scientific and educational organizations in the world. It reaches more than 285 million people worldwide each month through its official journal, NATIONAL GEOGRAPHIC, and its four other magazines; the National Geographic Channel; television documentaries; radio programs; films; books; videos and DVDs; maps; and interactive media. National Geographic has funded more than 8,000 scientific research projects and supports an education program combating geographic illiteracy.

For more information, please call 1-800-NGS LINE (647-5463) or write to the following address:

National Geographic Society
1145 17th Street N.W., Washington, D.C.
20036-4688 U.S.A.

Visit us online at
www.nationalgeographic.com/books

For librarians and teachers:
www.ngchildrensbooks.com

More for kids from National Geographic:
kids.nationalgeographic.com

For information about special discounts for bulk purchases, please contact National Geographic Books Special Sales: ngspecsales@ngs.org

For rights or permissions inquiries, please contact National Geographic Books Subsidiary Rights: ngbookrights@ngs.org

Library of Congress Cataloging-in-Publication Data available upon request

Hardcover ISBN: 978-1-4263-0361-6
Library ISBN: 978-1-4263-0327-2

Printed in China

Book design by Dan Banks, Project Design Company

### Published by the National Geographic Society

John M. Fahey, Jr., *President and Chief Executive Officer;* Gilbert M. Grosvenor, *Chairman of the Board;* Tim T. Kelly, *President, Global Media Group;* John Q. Griffin, *President, Publishing;* Nina D. Hoffman, *Executive Vice President; President, Book Publishing Group*

### Prepared by the Book Division

Nancy Laties Feresten, *Vice President, Editor in Chief, Children's Books;*
Bea Jackson, *Director of Design and Illustrations, Children's Books;*
Amy Shields, *Executive Editor, Series, Children's Books*

### Staff for This Book

Virginia Ann Koeth, *Editor*
Jim Hiscott, *Art Director*
Lori Epstein, *Illustrations Editor*
Stuart Armstrong, *Graphics*
Lewis R. Bassford, *Production Manager*
Grace Hill, *Associate Managing Editor*
Jennifer A. Thornton, *Managing Editor*
R. Gary Colbert, *Production Director*
Susan Borke, *Legal and Business Affairs*

### Manufacturing and Quality Management

Christopher A. Liedel, *Chief Financial Officer*
Phillip L. Schlosser, *Vice President*
Chris Brown, *Technical Director*
Nicole Elliott, *Manager*

### Photo Credits

Front cover: Edinburgh, Scotland, 1996: Dolly became the first animal to be cloned from DNA taken from an adult animal.

Back cover: model of DNA

Page 1: A Labradoodle puppy exhibits traits of both Labradors and poodles. Scientists created a hybrid breed in order to isolate the most desirable characteristics of both breeds.

Pages 2–3: Fluid samples for DNA analysis are dropped into a sample tray with a tool called a multichannel pipette.

### A Creative Media Applications, Inc. Production

Editor: Susan Madoff
Copy Editor: Laurie Lieb
Design and Production: Luís Leon and Fabia Wargin